"DADDY, WHY ARE YOU GOING TO JAIL?"

DADDY,
WHY ARE YOU GOING TO
JAIL?

STEPHEN P. LAWSON

Harold Shaw Publishers
Wheaton, Illinois

ISBN 0-87788-161-8

Cover design by David LaPlaca

Cover photo © 1992, Jim Wright

Library of Congress Cataloging-in-Publication Data

Lawson, Stephen P.
    "Daddy, why are you going to jail?" : a true story of a father's
  descent into white-collar crime and his amazing restoration /
  Stephen P. Lawson ; foreword by Chuck Colson.
      p.   cm.
    ISBN 0-87788-161-8
    1. Lawson, Stephen P.   2. Commercial criminals—United
  States—Biography.   3. White collar crimes—United States.
  4. Criminals—Rehabilitation—United States.   I. Title.
  HV6766.L39L39   1992
  364.1'68'092—dc20
    [B]   92-23261
                                                     CIP

---

99 98 97 96 95 94 93 92

10 9 8 7 6 5 4 3 2 1

This book tells of the faithfulness, mercy, and love of God. It also tells of the faithfulness, mercy, and love of my best friend, sister in Christ, wife, and the nicest person I have ever known—Elyse Harvey Lawson. My earnest prayer is that our son, Blake, might someday be blessed enough to marry as well as I have. Many others have contributed greatly in blessing our lives. You are known and appreciated by us and by our Lord. To Harvey, Blake, and all of you, this book is lovingly dedicated.

"May the LORD repay you for what you have done. May you be richly rewarded by the LORD, the God of Israel, under whose wings you have come to take refuge."
—Ruth 2:12

Contents

Foreword

With the recent twentieth anniversary of the Watergate break-in, I have been barraged with media requests and then interviewers' questions: As a White House conspirator, what was I thinking? Did I set out to break the law? No. One seemingly insignificant questionable decision led to another, until a federal prosecutor was asking big questions about a cover-up and I had little defense.

As the owner and president of a prominent Atlanta real estate investment firm, Steve Lawson let one rationalized shady "gamble" build on another until his world fell apart. Like thousands of other "white-collar criminals," he never suspected that someday he would plead guilty—before an earthly judge and, more important, before a heavenly Judge.

Sitting in the federal courtroom dock, Steve received no mercy from the bench—a stiff term in a federal prison camp.

But on his knees before his Maker, he found life-transforming power to face life and turn his back on plans for suicide; he found forgiveness and peace with God that would carry him through the trauma of incarceration.

I know what that word means for a man or woman who has a family. You're willing to pay the consequences for your own wrong-doing, but you can hardly bear the pain of knowing the hardship your actions have brought on your spouse, your children, your parents.

For offenders married when they enter prison, statistics are disheartening. Eighty-five percent of those prisoners will not have a spouse to return home to. Then another 10 percent of the marriages will not survive the first few years after the prisoner's release; the transition places too much stress on the family bond.

"Daddy, Why Are You Going to Jail?" is a book about a family's ability to walk forward into and through forgiveness. By the grace of God, Steve and his wife, Harvey, and their son, Blake, weathered the storm, choosing to cling to each other and to the God of second chances.

I first met Steve in 1980 when he was furloughed from the prison camp in Fort Walton Beach, Florida, to attend an intensive two-week Prison Fellowship seminar designed to disciple and give leadership skills to believers who would return to prison and minister to fellow inmates—the church behind bars.

At the closing "graduation," Steve's very countenance as he stood to speak briefly before the packed church was a testimony to God's work in and through him. For a time after his release he directed our Prison Fellowship work in the state of Georgia. He, like myself, could not easily walk away from the needs so evident in the lives of prisoners, ex-prisoners, and their families.

Steve and Harvey came to know God through the witness of friends and the piercing power of the two-edged Word of God. May the Holy Spirit use Steve's witness in these pages to touch the hearts of readers seeking a reason to live, a reason to forgive, even when bad choices—yours or someone else's—have set your life in a tailspin.

Chuck Colson
Chairman
Prison Fellowship

Preface

As this witness of my Lord and Savior Jesus Christ unfolds, it is my prayer it will tell of a life that has made a moral amendment in Jesus—the witness of a Jew who had his faith grow after crying out in a last desperate act of hope. A witness relating that in Jesus:

- Every adversity hides a beautiful possibility!
- You are able to be an important part of God's plan for that day!
- The Lord gives us dominion over our every limitation!
- Troubles can become triumphs!
- You can be in prison but not a prisoner!
- You are able to forgive and feel forgiven!
- Delay doesn't mean denial—especially of his love!

So in this book I open our lives to you with a great deal of enthusiasm because I am excited to share the faithfulness of a Lord who has dealt lovingly, with grace and mercy.

Stephen P. Lawson
Atlanta, Georgia
1992

Acknowledgments

For the most part, first-time authors without public name recognition have a difficult time getting published. My agent, Joyce Farrell, believed this autobiography needed to be shared and worked diligently in presenting the manuscript to various publishing houses. All the while she was a source of great encouragement to me.

Ramona Cramer Tucker is Director of Editorial Services at Harold Shaw Publishers and has been a pleasure to work with. Her belief in this manuscript was always heartening, and the talent and time she shared so liberally has allowed this story to be everything it was intended to be.

To both of these ladies, my family joins me in thanking you.

Many of the names in this story have been changed in order to protect privacy. Each name change is indicated by an asterisk (*) after its first occurrence.

Chapter 1

Good-bye, My Little Boy

Friday morning, March 2, 1979, started like any other day. The alarm buzzed at 6 A.M.

Harvey and I awoke at once. Our eyes met and said it all: *Is this really happening? Has today really arrived—the day we've dreaded?*

The last forty-five days had not prepared us for this moment. I had some knowledge of child psychology, but I could see how impossible it was going to be to put what little I knew into practice. How was I going to look at my son, Blake, and tell him what I had to say? Would the words even come out?

My wife Harvey tied the cloth belt to her robe, padded over to where I stood, and hugged me. "Oh, God," she whispered with tears in her throat, "Please be with Stephen and me. This is so tough. If we can make it for the next hour there won't be anything too hard to handle."

She started to walk away, but I reached to pull her close again. "Harvey, I love you *so much*. Honey, do you really understand that I'm another person now and how sorry I am for . . ." I couldn't finish, but she knew what I meant.

"I know," she replied. "It's just that right now it doesn't make things any easier. Please, Honey, I need to go to the kitchen. Can you get Blake dressed and ready for breakfast?"

Blake's ride to school was due in forty-five minutes. Harvey and I had agreed that we needed the extra fifteen minutes to break the news to him.

How do you tell the joy of your heart that you're going to prison? How is it possible to express how awful you feel and, at the same time, assure your son that everything will be okay—someday?

In recent weeks I had gone to Blake's room every evening after he'd fallen asleep and sat on the bed next to him. I would touch his beautiful child's features or stroke his hair. He was asleep and at peace. He knew nothing of how drastically his life was about to change. Most evenings I whispered to him the things that were on my heart, knowing he couldn't hear, much less understand.

"I'm sorry, Son." The words would struggle out as tears ran down my face. "Your mom and I waited to have a family for a long time—until everything was just right—and now look what I've done."

His breathing was regular and deep, the soft eyelashes still against his cheeks. The words kept spilling out, as much a prayer as an explanation. "You didn't ask to be born. You didn't count on this kind of heartbreak. I hope you won't be too scared over this and that you'll still be able to love and forgive me. If I knew you couldn't forgive me, Son, I'd honestly rather die."

Each night, while putting my hand on top of Blake's head, I would talk to my Father: *God, I don't even know how to pray for him, but I leave Blake with you and ask you to bless him in all ways, to protect him, and to love him through the tough times ahead. Oh, God, please don't let my failures become stumbling blocks in his young life.*

Later in bed—long after the lights were off and I could hear Harvey breathing rhythmically in sleep—I would pray for her in the stillness of the night. Life would be rough for her. Besides the burden of single parenting, there were the finances; I had no idea how she would make ends meet without any income from me.

I also prayed a lot for myself; I didn't know how I would survive eight years in prison.

Christian friends and members of various prayer groups around Atlanta knew of my upcoming sentence, and several attempted to give me encouragement: "Steve, what a wonderful ministry you can have there," or, "What a marvelous opportunity to get deeper into the Word." I couldn't help but think, somewhat facetiously, that if it weren't for the marvelous opportunities awaiting me in prison I'd really rather not go!

As each day passed and the commitment date loomed closer, the dark realities hit me with more awful force. My prayers for my son intensified as I fought panic. *Let him understand and not resent me. Don't allow him to feel abandoned . . . or to think that any of this could somehow be his fault.*

We had been advised on our dealings with Blake by a close friend, Liz,* who had several degrees in psychology and counseling. She said we must be completely honest with Blake. We agreed, as it would be difficult to convince even a five-year-old that his father would be out of town on business for a while—and stay away until he was nearly fourteen. Even if we weren't truthful, his classmates would be. I wanted the news to come from me. That much I could do for him, as little as it seemed to be.

Liz also stressed that it would be important for Blake to realize that I was going to a "camp" for daddies who had made mistakes, rather than a maximum security "slammer" type prison such as Blake had sometimes seen on television. "You must help him realize that you did not commit a violent crime," Liz emphasized. "And once he visits you he will feel better after seeing the environment. At this age,

Blake has no perception of time. If you tell him you'll be leaving in forty-five days, he'll have no idea of when that is. It would be silly—even cruel—to put him under any strain for that period of time. Better to prepare him by saying you will have to be leaving for a long time, sometime soon. Then, when you finally break the news, attempt to keep it as light as possible."

As light as possible? That would be the hardest part—to make it appear that everything would be all right while I crumbled inside. Prayer or no prayer, the pain of my coming separation from those I loved most was ever-present.

I decided to make the last days with Blake a time filled with good memories, closeness, and companionship. I hoped that the better part of eight years away would not wipe out special times we had always experienced together.

"Blake, how would you like to take one of your dad's best piggy-back rides?"

"Okay, Daddy, but don't move too fast until I get a good hold." He climbed up while I rested swaybacked on all fours. "Giddy-up horse!" he shouted gleefully.

I moved around the living room, occasionally bucking, speeding up, slowing down. All the while my heart was breaking.

"Oh, my, this old horse is getting tired. I think I'll stop over here and take a nap," I said softly.

"Be careful! I don't want to fall off!"

I slid to the carpet and lay on my stomach while Blake toppled off, then I rolled over to smother him in hugs and kisses while he squealed with delight.

"Blake, you know pretty soon Daddy is going to have to go away for a long time. I'm sure going to miss you. Are you going to miss me, too?"

"Uh-huh. I'll lift my arm up, and you see if you can tickle me under my arm before I put it down, okay?"

Obviously, he had heard me but had no idea what the words meant. The arm went up, his face gleaming with anticipation of how wonderful his newly made-up game would be. He was a bundle of little-boy energy in his red corduroy jumpsuit with the yellow Pooh Bear on front. I tickled him, and the most beautiful laughter in the world filled the room.

Lord, thank you for loving my little boy even more than I do. I hold you to your promise to never leave or forsake us—or to allow us to go through more than we can endure.

We were finally able to make Blake aware that on the following Friday his mom and I would go to Florida. The time had come to tell him that only his mom was making it round trip. Today was that day.

I went into Blake's room and began the regular wake-up routine. He lay on his stomach fast asleep.

"Good morning!" I called cheerfully as I rubbed his back and patted his rump through the blanket. "It's time to get up."

"Can I sleep a little longer?" he asked sleepily, as he did every morning, eyes still closed.

"You know it's a school day, and the car pool will pick you up in a little while. Come on. Up and at 'em."

Before long he was dressed and fed. Now wide awake, he played in his room, putting together the last pieces to a Donald Duck jigsaw puzzle.

Harvey and I walked into the room together. I sat on Blake's bed while Harvey stood, leaning on the dresser for support. I took a deep breath.

"Honey, put the puzzle down and come here for a minute. There's something Daddy has to tell you."

Blake put the last piece of the puzzle into place. Then he crossed the room and plopped down next to me on the bed, his short legs dangling a foot or so from the carpet.

He's so young. How in the world can I help him understand this? I agonized. He looked up at me. People have always said Blake looks a lot like me, but as I stared at him, he reminded me more of his mother, his eyes bluer than ever, the lashes incredibly long.

"What do you want to tell me?" he asked brightly. "Is it a surprise?"

"Do you remember how Daddy has said many times that he might have to go away for a l-o-n-g time?"

"Yes." He nodded, his eyes full of questions.

"Well, Daddy is going to drive to a place in Florida today and—"

"Oh boy! Can I go, too? Please, Daddy?" he squealed with delight. He jumped off the bed and faced me, all smiles. "When are we going to go? What will we do in Florida?"

"Son, wait a minute. Sit back up here next to me on the bed."

As Blake climbed up on the bed again I stole my first glance at Harvey. I had never seen so much sorrow in her face. Her keen blue eyes watered, and her drawn features seemed transfixed in watching a heart-breaking event. I knew how powerless she felt. Our eyes met. She bit her lip and slowly shook her head.

I turned back to Blake, feeling like I couldn't breathe. My next statement would change his world. "Daddy is going to drive to a place in Florida today, with Mommie and Liz." I spoke quickly, compulsively, not inviting interruptions. "I'll have to stay there a long time, but I want you to know that I love you and Mommie with all my heart and that I'm going to be counting the days until I can come home again so we can be a family."

His eyes, like mine, filled with tears.

"Daddy, don't go—"

"Son, I don't *want* to go, but I *have* to."

6

"Why?"

"Daddy made a . . . mistake in business and broke the law. You know how Daddy has to punish you when you're naughty?"

He nodded solemnly.

"Well, it's the same thing when you're grown up—even when you're a daddy. I did some things that were wrong . . . very wrong . . . so I went to court where a judge told me I had to go to a place called a work camp, along with other daddies who have made mistakes. I'll have to stay there a long time."

"No!" he cried, the tears gushing down his face now. "Don't go, Daddy! Tell him I don't want you to go!"

I knew that the ocean of tears I had held back all those times we played couldn't be stayed now for more than another sixty seconds. "Boy, I'm going to miss you and Mommie," I finished, in a vain effort to keep my voice light.

"What did you do wrong?" Blake asked through his tears.

How could I possibly explain security violations and mail fraud to him? "It's hard for me to explain to you right now," I said, haltingly. "But I *didn't* hurt anybody, and it isn't like anything you see on TV police programs. I've never done anything like that. Someday when you're older and you can understand better, I'll tell you all about it."

Blake slid to the floor and planted himself in front of me, looking up with glistening eyes. "You can tell me *now*. I'm a *big* boy. I'm five years old, you know."

I pulled him close so that I wouldn't have to look into his eyes anymore. The sobs started. They began in my stomach, worked themselves into my throat, and wrenched out of my mouth in sounds I'd never heard before. My body convulsed, but I could not allow myself to give in.

Harvey came to my rescue with marvelous voice control. "Everything will be fine. We are a family, and we love one another." She got on her knees and took Blake's two hands in her own, gazing deeply into his eyes. "Blake, Darling, everything is going to be okay. Daddy and I both love you, and Daddy and I love each other."

"But I don't want him to go," he sobbed.

"I know—I don't either. But we'll visit him often. As a matter of fact, how would you like to go to Florida with me in about two weeks to visit him?"

"Okay. But I still don't want him to go."

She embraced him. "I know." Her blue eyes locked with mine. This hadn't gone well, but somehow it was over. We had told him, and he knew. We didn't have to dread the event anymore.

I knelt down beside them, tears still streaming down my face. "I guess I'm the most blessed person in the world to have a family like you guys." I smiled as best I could. "You know, the amount of time I have to spend away won't compare to all the years we'll have together as a family when this is all over. I love you Blake, and I'm very proud of you."

A horn sounded from the driveway. Blake's ride with three other children his age waited for him.

"Of all mornings to be early!" I said with manufactured cheeriness. Harvey dried her tears and blotted Blake's face so she could take him downstairs.

As they were going out the front door Blake turned and bolted back up the stairs to me. I picked him up and hugged him, feeling his smooth cheek against mine.

"I love you, Daddy."

"I love you, too, Son. Be Dad's best boy and listen to your mother while I'm gone. Promise?"

"I promise."

"I'm going to write you every day, so watch for the mail. I'm even going to address the envelopes to *you*." I hoped that the forced smile and upbeat voice were convincing.

Harvey and Blake went downstairs while I walked over to the window and watched. After a half minute of small talk with Harvey, the driver pulled out. I watched the car disappear around the bend on Peachtree Road. By then, Harvey had returned. She draped her arm across my back.

There was nothing to say, so we stood quietly for a few moments. I had just watched half my heart leave, and I wasn't at all sure what was going on inside my son. I couldn't move away from the window.

"I only wish I could be Blake for the next hour or so," I murmured. "Then I'd know exactly what is going through his mind. It would help us know what to do—to make it easier for him somehow."

Harvey's arm dropped to my waist and I turned, squeezing her close to me.

"Heavenly Father," she prayed, "Stephen and I pray that any trauma, bitterness, or lack of understanding Blake might feel will be openly expressed and in no way suppressed. Father, give me wisdom and love to deal with Blake during these days and years ahead. Show me what he needs and give me the ability to deal with it. But Lord, please be with Blake now and send guardian angels to give him comfort. Let him know that we are a blessed family who love each other, but most of all love you."

Shortly afterward, Liz arrived. We packed the car, and I asked them to remain downstairs while I took one last private tour of our apartment. Slowly I passed from room to room, looking at objects I particularly loved, remembering each occasion they represented.

I walked into the living room and was drawn to the formal portrait of my father. Dad had died fourteen years earlier. When he was alive, I had considered him a friend as well as my father. "How I wish you were here today, Dad," I said under my breath. Then I checked myself. "It's probably better this way, though. Why live to the age you would have been now, only to have this grief kill you?"

My father's life had been a difficult one. At one time he had been a wealthy man and had the respect, perhaps even envy, of many. Then his business had failed. He lost money, people's respect, and his good-time friends. Dad also lost his wife, even though they existed together until he died.

Mom had never recovered from the pressure and the strain. She held considerable bitterness toward many people, including Dad. In the photograph I held in my hands, Dad looked at peace. As my eyes rested on his, it was as though he had, for the moment, come alive. I experienced a deep love and understanding from him that I had never known before.

The tears flowed openly. "Dad, forgive me for the shame I've brought to the Lawson name," I whispered. "I really loved you, but because of the way things were at home I guess I never got around to telling you."

I sat down heavily on the sofa and caved in with sobs again. This pain seemed like it would go on forever. But it seemed important to continue this talk I was having with Dad. I cradled his picture in one hand. In the quietness of the room, it was as though he lived and could hear everything I said through my sobs.

"Dad, I have a son now whom you never got to meet. He's a fine boy. You would have liked him, and I would have loved to see you be a grandfather to him." I sat still while the hurricane rocked inside me. "Where is all this going to end, Dad? I've lost my money the same as you. My old friends have disappeared just like yours did."

Then, for some moments, I spoke to my heavenly Father, begging him not to allow Blake to be the victim of a victim the way I had been. *Break this chain. Condition his little heart not to feel resentment toward me and to love me in spite of the bad decisions I've made*, I prayed, for God's ears alone.

I turned back to Dad's picture. "The most important thing in my life right now is for Blake to be able to forgive me—and I have a lot more in my life to be forgiven of than you did. . . ." Suddenly, for the first time in my life, I knew why I had wrestled so much with my relationship with my dad. "I never really forgave *you*," I said. No one in our family had ever said, "I'm sorry," for anything, and no one had ever spoken words of forgiveness. Sorrowfully, I began to forgive my father—for the times he hadn't been there, for not being interested enough in my life, for never expressing pride in my accomplishments. I forgave him for not standing his ground with my mother, for allowing her anger to control our household. One by one, the grievances came to mind, and I said, "Dad, I forgive you." Then I saw with startling clarity the ways in which I had wronged him and my mother. With each remembrance, I asked, "Please forgive *me* . . ."

Finally, I wiped my face. I was cleansed. Something wonderful had just taken place; I knew that God had been—was still—present in the room. I returned Dad's picture to its place and picked up a picture of Harvey and me taken at the Southampton Princess Hotel in Bermuda. What a happy time we'd had. Would we ever know times like that again? Was there a way that one could pick up the pieces and start new dreams? Would the long years away wear out Harvey's resolve and love for me? Would we still be a family when it was all over, as we'd both promised our son? Even if Harvey didn't leave me, would our relationship become like that of *my* parents?

I thrust away the dark doubts, for I knew that Harvey's and my life together was quite different from what my parents' had been. God had already freed me from an infinitely harsher—if invisible—prison. Surely he would walk with us both during our years of confinement. Harvey serving her sentence, me serving mine.

I drank in every detail of my home, wondering how many treasured possessions would have to be sold off for pennies on the dollar so that Harvey could put food on the table. So many things truly were in God's hands now; every power had been stripped from me.

Lord, this is too much for me to handle. I can't bear it without your help. With that final cry for assistance, I clapped my hands together in much the same way football players do when a huddle is broken. I took a last look around, then walked out the door.

Harvey would later recall:

I know the Lord says that we should only concern ourselves with the events of today, since tomorrow has enough worries of its own. At that awful moment it was easy to do the scriptural thing. The present was so painful and the future so bleak and uncertain that I couldn't contemplate trying to think past the day. Tomorrow seemed years away. I was like a piece of driftwood caught in a current of a turbulent river, along for the ride. I didn't ask to be thrown into the river; I was truly an innocent victim of Stephen's past actions. Would Blake and I be able to continue to live in our residence? Would I have to move in with my mother or Aunt Francine? How long would Stephen be away? What in the world was going to become of us? My questions and concerns were endless.

Chapter 2

A Change of Address

Perhaps no other place is so lovely as Atlanta in March, as it heralds the beginning of spring. Jonquils, crocuses, dogwood trees, and azalea bushes awaken after a winter's rest and bloom in profusion. And that day, no one appreciated them more than I did. As we drove through Atlanta, heading south, I devoured all the sights, especially our immediate neighborhood. I wanted to remember everything in vivid detail; years would pass before I would ever see it again.

We drove most of the seven hours with little conversation. Our thoughts centered on Blake, yet we had nothing new to say. So we sat with our private thoughts and didn't try to force conversation.

Because of Liz's generous offer, we stayed at a beautiful Destin condo that overlooked a golf course. We bought shrimp at a local fishmarket for our evening meal and cooked it ourselves. We wanted to be close to the phone. We had prearranged to call Blake at 7:30 P.M. to find out how he was handling my being gone. And on our part we wanted to furnish an upbeat, positive report.

For that weekend we had left Blake with friends of ours whose children Blake enjoyed. We wanted to believe he was having a wonderful time. We had been careful not to mention the word "prison," saying, "work camp" instead. We decided that when Blake came to visit he could draw his own conclusions. After all, we hadn't seen the place ourselves and couldn't describe it to him.

Finally, it was time to call. My stomach tightened, and I felt myself perspire in the air-conditioned room. I started to dial, got mixed up in the middle, and slowly redialed. The wife answered.

"Hey, Betty,* it's Steve. How's everything going?"

"Not very well, really—wait a minute. I'd like Bill* to speak with you."

When Bill picked up the phone, he didn't pause to greet me. "Blake is distraught. He's right here and needs to talk with you."

"Okay," I said fearfully, "put him on."

"Daddy, why are you going to jail?"

He will never know how those sobbed-out words cut into my heart. He could only assume that I had lied to him. I wondered how a five-year-old could bear the pain he was feeling. I wanted to reach through the telephone wire and hold him. Unprepared for his question, I nearly dropped the phone and started to cry, myself.

"No, Blake. I'm calling from Florida at a place where Mommie, Liz, and I are staying." Even though my voice sounded under control, my body shook. Anger flooded through me. We had told our friends how we chose to handle the situation. Apparently they had shown no respect for our judgment. Who had mentioned "prison" to Blake?

"Daddy, Janey told me you're going to prison. Are you going to *jail*?"

"Son, it's like I told you this morning. Daddy did some things wrong in business, and I'm going to a place in Florida for punishment. It's not a jail—not a *real* jail—but some people might call it that. It's a work camp for daddies who have made mistakes."

"Then you *are* going to prison, aren't you? What did you do?" The sound of betrayal careened through the line.

"Honey, please don't cry—" I couldn't restrain my own tears any longer, and I handed the phone to Harvey. What more could I possibly say? How could he absorb even the best explanation? No judge in the world could have imposed a tougher sentence on me than the one that had just transpired.

Harvey spoke to Blake for about ten minutes with generous assistance from Liz and ended with, "We'll call you tomorrow. Dad and I love you more than anything in the world, and things aren't nearly as bad as you think. Will you please put Mrs. Ramsey* on the phone again?"

Then to Betty, she said, "If Blake has any more rough times between now and the time we're scheduled to call tomorrow, phone us here right away, no matter the hour."

Betty secured our number, assuring Harvey that they hadn't been the ones to upset Blake. Harvey was courteous but didn't sound as though she believed that. After she had hung up the phone, Harvey and I held each other tightly.

Putting an arm around each of us, Liz prayed softly, asking for God's peace for us, for Blake, and for the Ramseys.

After that, both Harvey and I relaxed. I had some trouble getting to sleep, but I kept reminding myself that I could do nothing to change the situation. Nevertheless, Blake's face came to me again and again, the one showing his current pain as well as the happy face of the times before this day.

To our relief, we learned the next morning that he'd done fine and was already out swimming. We also learned how

Blake had heard the word "prison." One of the little girls had prayed for me. For a long while I'd been the object of family prayer in that household. The words had slipped out, something entirely unavoidable, and the child didn't realize at the time that she had done anything wrong.

We had long planned for this particular Saturday. Harvey and I took a long walk on the beach, talking and praying. The touch of her hand on mine was a great reassurance.

Later, we drove out to the prison camp to see how it looked.

As we approached the prison camp, conversation in the car died. Even Liz, who was driving, had retreated into silence. Just how bad could bad be? This was the place where the courts said I would spend the better part of eight years.

We could hardly believe what we saw. *It was beautiful.* Bright green, neatly trimmed lawns surrounded a complex that looked much more like a small college campus than a prison. It had none of the towers, barbed wire, or high walls associated with prison life.

We immediately thought of Blake and were thrilled that he would see me here, in such a nonthreatening atmosphere. We quickly agreed that he and Harvey would make the trip in two weeks, giving me time to get acclimated. By the time we drove away the atmosphere in the car had changed considerably. The tension was still present, but the future had taken on tangible proportions, which were easier to deal with than imaginations gone wild.

Since it took seven hours to drive from Ft. Walton Beach to Atlanta, with another hour added because of the time difference, we decided that Harvey and Liz would leave me around noon during the church service the next day. That way they could pick up Blake by eight o'clock that night.

We had arranged to meet a couple a friend of ours had told us about at St. Andrews-by-the-Sea Episcopal Church. Long-time members there, Rick and Dottie had an incredible ministry of hospitality. They had offered to bring me home from church with them and later drop me off at Eglin Federal Prison Camp. Although we had never met before, they had agreed to open their home and their lives to me, a complete stranger, after the long-distance introduction of a mutual friend.

Saturday night, as Harvey and I lay in bed together for what we knew would be the last time for a long while, reality hit us. We could only hold one another, and keep repeating that we loved each other.

I have since learned that fear indicates a faith in the enemy's ability, but that evening I *was* fearful. Every worry came to me at once. How would Harvey and Blake make it financially? Would Blake be okay? Could Harvey handle the loneliness? The rejection? Would our marriage—*could* our marriage—survive?

How long would I be away? Would I be safe? I'd heard stories. How real was the chance of being beaten . . . or raped?

In the silent room, as the hour grew later, Harvey had her own thoughts and questions, some too personal, I imagined, even to share with me. That troubled me, because I wanted to share every thought, every breath.

Harvey's and my strength since becoming Christians was in privately talking with God, in quietness. Yet we both realized our need for more human contact, and were always able to air distraught feelings and receive comfort from God and each other, too.

Finally, my hand on hers, I drifted off to sleep. I didn't wake up until morning.

St. Andrews-by-the-Sea afforded Harvey, Liz, and me the sort of worship each of us needed. St. Andrew's has a memorable choir, one of the most beautiful I'd ever heard. As the service progressed, Harvey and I held hands, not daring to look at one another for fear of crying.

Before the service concluded, the three of us slipped out of church, walking slowly toward the car in an attempt to stall our good-byes. Liz walked several paces ahead, allowing us what privacy she could.

It was so impossible! *How in the world am I going to say good-bye to Harvey?* Surely this wasn't happening! It was a bad dream, and Harvey would shake me awake and say, "Stephen, are you all right? You were crying out in your sleep."

I reached inside the car and picked up a large paper sack that held the few things we assumed they'd allow me to take into the prison. I quickly kissed Harvey good-bye, thanked Liz for all her help, then assisted them into the car. I kept taking deep breaths. It had hurt and been rough, but we had handled it well.

I turned, walked away, and was within a few steps of the church door when I saw the car begin to pull away. Suddenly the tears came. Springs erupted from the places my eyes were meant to occupy.

The car passed, and I saw the face of a person I had loved with all my heart from almost the first moment I met her. Now she was being carried away from a husband who had promised to love and provide for her.

I stopped, unable to enter the church because of my uncontrolled sobbing. A few years earlier I'd had every material thing a person could ask from life—expensive cars, a beautiful home, closets filled with good clothes, wonderful vacations. Now, I stood in an unfamiliar parking lot clutching a paper bag filled with just a few possessions that remained from my old life: a pair of tennis shoes, sweat socks, my Bible, and shaving gear.

I felt completely empty, without hope. The enormous pain of the past and the tragedy of the present hit me as never before. At that moment there seemed to be nothing to hope for. I had no future.

Then the car stopped, and backed up. Harvey ran to me in an instant, and I buried my face in the crook of her neck.

"Please don't cry, Honey," she said. It sounded like she was begging. "Everything will be okay. I love you so much."

I nodded, my face still pressed against her, unable to speak.

"If you make it back into church, I know you'll feel better," she said.

I nodded, and we kissed. We didn't allow our eyes to meet. She got into the car, and they began to drive away. My emotions gave way again, and the scene was repeated, her coming to me, speaking words of assurance, her lingering embrace, the loving good-bye. This time I managed to regain enough composure to walk back into the church.

Who started the rumor that women are the weaker sex? As I relive that parting scene, I still marvel at Harvey's strength. She was much stronger than I. Strong enough that I could draw strength from her.

Once inside the church, I dropped my paper bag beside the door and crept into a pew near the back. The serving of Holy Communion began. The choir sang softly and people from the front rows advanced toward the altar to kneel. Because of the size of the congregation, I knew it would be only a few minutes before my turn came.

I thought the worst was over, but the pain returned and so did the tears. I felt helpless, awkward, foolish, wondering what people would think of the sobbing stranger in the back pew. But mostly I missed Harvey and wanted to touch her, to take communion with her. I wanted my best friend. When the usher stood at my pew I could hardly make the effort, but the whole row of people waited for me.

My handkerchief never left my face. I knelt to receive the elements that symbolize our Lord's broken body and his blood. The priests offered me the sacraments. A woman knelt beside me. I felt her soft hand on mine, holding it tightly. I returned the grasp. It seemed that God had sent the woman by proxy, for Harvey. Here was the hand I needed, the strength from another person. I was not alone.

Since that time, I have thought of the biblical story of a woman who anointed Jesus' head with costly perfume. It seemed a small act—even a foolish one, to some people—but Jesus had said, " . . . wherever this gospel is preached throughout the world, what she has done will also be told, in memory of her" (Matthew 26:13). In that same spirit I will always remember Carolyn, the woman who comforted me by her touch.

The two priests, knowing nothing about me and yet sensitive to the crisis of the moment, came over and rested their hands tenderly on my head and prayed. Those prayers, and especially Carolyn's hand, brought me to a place of peace. I didn't need to cry anymore. As I knelt there in that Episcopal church, surrounded by strangers—yet brothers and sisters in the faith—the Lord provided the kind of inner strength I needed. I could even offer a weak smile to those around me.

A few moments later, the worship service ended. Parishioners adjourned to an adjacent building for coffee and fellowship. I went there and sought out the Culps, the man and wife my friend had told me about. Since they both sang in the choir, we had arranged to meet after the service. Warm and open people, they immediately welcomed me.

After a short while I felt amazingly well—and loved. Sorrow and guilt for myself was in the distance; my concern centered around Harvey. She had a long drive from Destin to Atlanta, and she was returning to some heavy responsibilities. I was relieved she was with Liz rather than making the trip alone. I knew that for me this period of peace and composure was God's grace and sent up a silent prayer of thanks, knowing he would afford Harvey the same gift.

Harvey was suffering fears of her own:

As we drove away from that church, my head throbbed with pain. I instinctively rubbed my forehead and temples, trying to rub the hurt away, but no relief could be found. The sunlight hurt my eyes so I closed them, but I knew rest would be impossible.

Fear translated itself to a tightness in my chest and shortness of breath. I directed the air conditioner vent to my face. Liz was considerate enough not to talk and invade my turmoil, so at least I didn't have to process my thoughts for conversation.

In just forty-eight hours my life had fallen apart. I had watched my little boy say good-bye to the father he adores. Now, on a more adult level, I was saying good-bye to my very best friend. Could this be happening? I cried silently. At the same time, I told myself that I must maintain control, pull myself together. I had too much responsibility; I had to be a good witness. But that was stupid! I wasn't capable of anything—outside of God's intervening. I prayed desperately just to be able to make it through. I begged for God's help. Without realizing it, I turned Stephen over to God's care at that moment. I couldn't begin to carry his pain as well as my own.

After brunch the Culps took me home with them. Rick and I spent the afternoon walking and chatting on the beach. After dinner, we drove to hear the St. Andrews-by-the-Sea choir sing at a neighboring church. And then they drove me to Eglin, my work camp—and home—for the years ahead.

In the car I asked, "Rick, would you do me a favor and call Harvey when you get home? She should be in Atlanta in another hour. When she left I was a mess. Would you tell her that I'm all right? *Really* all right!"

"Of course." He smiled and patted my shoulder. "I had planned to call anyway."

I thanked him for that kindness. "And tell her that although the day started as the worst day of my life, after Communion and my afternoon with you and Dottie, it became one of the nicest, most tranquil days in my memory."

"That's wonderful," Rick said. "Do you want us to tell her anything else?"

"Just tell her that somehow I feel ready to go now. I feel prepared for whatever the future holds."

The headlights brought my new home-away-from-home into view. In another moment we parked. Rick, Dottie, and I shared a brief prayer. Then I headed inside. As I waved good-bye, I was at peace.

Chapter 3

On the Inside

"Okay, Lawson, pick up that pile of clothes over there and follow me," barked the guard.

"Yes, sir," I answered. "Do you want me to change now?"

"Lawson, when I want you to change clothes I'll *tell* you to change clothes. I *said* 'follow me.' Are you going to follow me or stand there and ask a lot of stupid questions? You might have been a big shot on the outside, but that crap doesn't fly here. Understand?"

"Yes, sir."

I followed him to a small room that contained shelves of blankets and sheets on one wall and hanging rods of civilian clothes on the other two.

"Okay, Lawson," said the guard as he sat down on the only chair in the room, "strip down and stand in front of me when you've finished."

I undressed and stood three feet in front of him. The guard, making no effort to disguise his personal disdain toward all prisoners and perhaps the tough breaks he had endured to have to take a job like this, stood up, toe to toe with me. As he gave his next command I would feel the warmth and smell the foul odor of his nicotine breath.

"Put your hands over your head."

Without comment, I complied. His hands ran over my body and through my hair. He made it a point to look closely at all major veins to determine if I mainlined drugs.

I had played basketball all through school, and even as an adult had been in many locker rooms and never considered myself particularly modest. But this process went beyond a matter of modesty; it was dehumanizing. He didn't miss an inch of my body. "Bend over!" He picked up a flashlight and inspected my rectum. I found out later that all prisoners are treated that way, in order to prevent their smuggling in drugs.

The strongest possible statement about my role as a prisoner had been made by this initiation. Within minutes I *knew* I had left my old life behind. I had lost ordinary rights. I learned quickly that I was in prison and under the total authority of others. For whatever time I was there I would be subject to the authority of guards who had a life sentence of their own and had become horribly jaded in the process. Prisoners would serve their time and go home. The guards, however, stayed on with no time off for good behavior. Almost every contact with them indicated the same thought process: We were there *to be punished* as opposed to being there *as punishment.*

Then came the rest of the process—mug shots, giving personal information. It was assembly-line automatic. Another guard assigned me a cot, then sheets, blankets, and pillowcases. I dressed in my prison clothing issue of steel-toed shoes, secondhand blue Air Force shirts and pants, tee shirts, socks, and underwear.

Since it was eleven at night, long past lights out, I had to make my bed in the dark, stuffing my other new possessions in a foot locker alongside. I guessed about thirty people slept in the barracks. Large fans stirred the stale, humid air. The loud droning of the fans combined with snoring noises from around the room provided an alien, disconcerting backdrop for my first night's sleep.

I lay on my back, thinking. Harvey, Blake, and I recently had begun a fabulous walk with God. I even felt a strange sort of prospective excitement about the sort of credibility our witness would bring, secure in the knowledge of knowing it wasn't where you served that mattered—but *who* you served.

I knew I belonged to the Lord. Jesus Christ had taken me into protective custody. Rather than "doing time," time would become my ally. I silently pledged myself to learning God's Word so that one day, when I left, I would be a lot stronger than when I arrived. I also had the assurance that even though Harvey and I were apart, prison could not truly separate us any more than it could separate me from the love of Jesus Christ.

With this assurance I prayed for my family, then slipped into a solid sleep, broken only hours later by a gruff voice over a loud speaker that heralded in my first day "on the inside."

As the others got out of bed I noticed they left their beds unmade. Not knowing what to do or where to go, I decided to copy the movements of others. I quickly dressed in the clothes I had taken off the night before and grabbed for my toilet articles. I followed the traffic pattern to a large bathroom that contained two dozen sinks, with as many urinals and bath stalls.

A wave of nausea hit me as I stared at the room. The floors were filthy, the garbage containers overflowing, and most sinks covered with bits of hair and soap-scum rings. The subdued atmosphere prevailed with hardly a word passing between the men. Each person was trying to focus his eyes and get started for the day.

I shaved and washed my face and hands quickly and, still following the traffic pattern, made my way back to my cot. No one had yet made his bed and I vaguely wondered why, because I felt reasonably sure that no one else would come in to do it. The traffic moved ahead and out of the building. I followed.

I was totally alone. I knew no one. Steve Lawson, the super-salesman, the man always at ease with people, now didn't know how to get acquainted and break the ice. That had never stopped me before when I went into a room filled with strangers. But it was different now. Everything was different. Worst of all, I didn't know any of the rules.

I was half afraid to make any associations. Suppose the person I spent time with was disliked by others and it made me guilty by association? Would I be safe here? Several inmates gave me the impression they could get quite physical if the situation called for it. Over the past few months I had heard many pitiful tales of violence and rape. What would it be like in the showers? I saw an immediate dilemma. I didn't want to shower with a crowd of others, but on the other hand I didn't want to be caught alone in there either.

As I followed the flow of men, all my worst fears came back. Every terrible worry hit as if for the first time. How would I survive here for the better part of eight years? How could Harvey and Blake make it on the outside? Would I even have a family once all this was over? Would it ever *really* be over? My heart crashed inside me like a sledge-hammer.

We came into the mess hall and, for the first time, the men talked among themselves. I ate in silence and listened to the general comments of other prisoners. Many found fault with everything and everyone. No one said a word to me. And, for the first time in my life, I said nothing to a single person—there in that mess hall filled with about 350 men, seated at tables for four. I was surprised to find that the breakfast included a good menu that featured pancakes.

Some of the inmates seemed to be in good spirits, and the guards acted friendly enough, although aloof.

Then it was back to the barracks for bed-making, orientation lectures, a tour of the compound, followed by a literacy test, physical exam, and job assignment.

———◆———

My first two weeks at Eglin revolved around barracks duty of cleaning urinals, vacuuming floors, cleaning windows, and emptying garbage cans. The free enterprise system does not exist in prison, and every inmate moves at a snail's pace. I tried to do my work cheerfully. I don't know how well I succeeded, but I kept asking God to give me strength and not to let me feel sorry for myself. I also knew that it had to get better.

But on that first day, I realized something that would help me do time much more easily. It's a simple concept, but it made the difference for me: *Nothing about the system ever seems reasonable*. At that moment, I determined not to let illogical and unfair things bother me. I now lived in an illogical and unreasonable world. I asked God for a generous sense of humor so I could see the comical side of things. In time, that decision would prove invaluable.

Chapter 4

Celebrations

Prison allows plenty of time for introspection, and I thought a great deal about my earlier life and all that had gone on before. Naturally, I thought about all the mistakes I had made. But I thought a lot about my family, too, and about growing up—about the reasons I had made the decisions I did.

First of all, I believe that each person is responsible for his or her own choices. I went to prison for acts *I* committed, knowing full well that I had been wrong. I would never lay my guilt at the feet of my parents or anyone else. But it can be a healing and helpful process to understand the difficulties and hurts of life, and to see how those things have impacted your life. It's been said that a person lives at home for his first eighteen years and then uses the rest of his life attempting to deal with those years. A few significant events in my background helped shape me into the Stephen Lawson who married Harvey, fathered Blake, and had a lot of business success, then lost it all and went to prison . . .

I was born to Sanford and Lillian Lawson in 1937. It was the second marriage for each and, in retrospect, appeared happy as long as my father remained successful. For my first ten years, I remember Dad as a successful dress manufacturer with office/showrooms in New York City and mills in Worcester, Massachusetts. We lived on a beautiful estate in Kings Point, near Long Island Sound.

Our family included Rosemary, my sister from Mother's first marriage. Rosemary is twelve years older than I, and I didn't know she was my half-sister until I was thirteen. I just thought of her as the faultless sister, the one I was expected to emulate in personality, manners, and schoolwork. Rosemary and I laugh at that today, because she recalls a lot of parental discipline for someone considered so perfect.

Since I was ten or eleven when Rosemary married Arthur and moved away, we didn't grow up very close. Our parents, until the year Rosemary married, enjoyed a great deal of prosperity. They entertained lavishly and kept our stately home crowded with guests.

Rosemary remembers Dad as the dominant parent. Her memories recall him as demanding, even authoritarian, and not particularly understanding or considerate. She points out that he was short, uneducated, and came from England without a dime in his pocket, yet had made it big. He wore his success like an upperclass Englishman wears his school tie. He ordered Mother around as if she were an underling created to carry out his commands.

Since Dad had lost all his money by the time I turned thirteen, my life—and perceptions of my parents—differed considerably from Rosemary's. After Dad's business losses came his heart problems, and later his strokes. His financial failures also took their toll. The Dad I knew was a lamb compared to the lion of Rosemary's memory. I'd always considered him the victim, whereas she had seen him as the villain.

I pictured Mother as the dominant person in our household. She was a tiger! A wounded tiger, doubtless, with an accumulation of hurts and scars that caused her to attack the ones she loved—especially her husband and her son.

During my early years on the estate, though, life was uncomplicated and most enjoyable. I went to summer camp in New Hampshire, had long romps with my collie on our spacious lawn, and played with many friends. Despite the dreamlike quality of those times, however, I felt that something was wrong—something I couldn't consciously identify.

My seventh birthday party brought these feelings sharply into focus. Dad and Mother went to enormous trouble and expense. There were Uncle Remus characters molded from ice cream, multi-colored balloons, and a magician's act. The extensive guest list included children of my parents' friends, plus a few of my schoolmates.

I had already begun to realize the importance of impressions. My parents taught by example. They always associated with the right people and encouraged me to be friendly with their children. The public school I attended also had children of less privileged circumstances. I should have been thrilled about the party my parents had planned for me. But even at age seven I knew that the party was as much for their benefit as mine.

I still have vivid memories of my guests arriving. Kids my age, well polished, dressed in their best party clothes, came in, each with a beautifully wrapped present, and handed it to me as my folks and I greeted them at the door.

Of all the guests, I wanted to see Jane Bullock* most of all. To me, she was the most beautiful girl who had ever lived, and I imagined that we would grow up and get married someday. I explained my feelings to my parents as we stood by the door, and I begged them not to ask what her father did or where they lived. Jane's father had died, and she and her mother lived in a modest apartment behind the post office in nearby Great Neck. I knew there was a difference between their situation and ours, and I didn't want her to feel out of place.

Someone in an old car let Jane off at the base of our driveway. She was not dressed as richly as the other children. But she still looked great to me. She didn't have a boxed gift, but handed me a birthday card. Inside the envelope she had placed a brand new one-dollar bill.

"Hello, Honey," my mother said and then commented on how pretty Jane looked and how pleased she was to meet her. Her tone of voice did not make the comments sound believable. I felt awful.

It got even worse. "Where do you live, Honey?" Mother continued, and, "What does your father do?" I was totally embarrassed and humiliated for Jane—and furious with my mother.

That night I took the dollar Jane had given me and wrote "I love Jane Bullock. May 24, 1944" across the face.

Seventeen years later, on a Saturday night, I happened to be back in that old neighborhood on business. At day's end, I took some time to reminisce as I drove by old landmarks. I was amazed to find my favorite delicatessen still in business and stopped in for a corned beef sandwich.

As I savored the mingled scents of Kosher pickles, salamis, and myriad other meats and spices in that place, I noticed a couple about my age who sat several tables over. The woman was facing me, and I was jolted with recognition. On impulse, I walked over to them.

"Excuse me," I said. "I don't mean to interrupt. But are you Jane Bullock, by any chance?"

"It used to be," she smiled, "but now it's Westmoreland*".

"I'm Steve Lawson, and—"

"Oh my gosh! Jason*, this is Steve Lawson. We were in first grade together, and I was crazy about him. I almost died when he moved away." Jason laughed good-naturedly at Jane's animated introduction and invited me to join them.

I sat down, and Jane and I recalled old times. Before long, she brought up that long-ago birthday party. "It was the most beautiful party I have ever been to in my entire life."

I stared in disbelief. All those years, I'd carried the hurt of that moment when she had walked through our door and was met by Mother's inquisition. Yet Jane's memory was completely different. It was a moment she had never remembered and one I had never forgotten. Then I noticed she was wearing a corsage. She explained that it was her birthday.

"If I'd known we would meet tonight," I said, "I would have bought a present for you, with the hope that you would love it as much as I loved the present you gave me. Do you remember that present?"

"You're embarrassing me, Steve. I have no idea."

I reached inside my sport jacket for my pocket secretary, fished in one of its compartments, and pulled out the dollar bill. I handed it to Jane.

She opened the folded bill and stared down at what was undeniably the handwriting of a seven-year-old "I love Jane Bullock. May 24, 1944." When she looked up again there were tears in her eyes.

When I was twelve, we moved to Worcester. That move ended an era. We lived there no longer than three years, yet I recall that period with sadness, because by then Dad knew he was out of business and broke. During that period, I, unnoticed at the top of the stairway in our rented house on Beechmont Road, often listened to my parents' conversations about divorce.

At times Mother vented her frustration at him through furious tirades at me, making terrible and untrue accusations about my conduct and lack of honesty. Many times she would corner me and shout, "You're just like your father! You're going to end up just like him!" I resented her slandering my father, and I hated her accusations against me. Although falsely accused, I was helpless to rebut her. It became clear that Dad had a wife he didn't care for, and that I had a mother I didn't much like, either. The yelling became a pattern of life.

I was to be Bar Mitzvahed in Worcester on my thirteenth birthday. My folks, not being particularly religious, had never expressed any interest in my fulfilling that Jewish ritual, but it was something I wanted to do badly. Accordingly, they arranged for me to take Hebrew lessons six months before the big date. Three days a week I walked over to Rabbi Bernstein's* house after school.

The rabbi lived in a modest neighborhood in an unpretentious white house with a wrap-around porch. Inside, the Bernsteins kept the boxy rooms dimly lit, with lace doilies of various shapes and sizes carefully placed on every available flat surface.

Mrs. Bernstein was a stout woman with a sweet, if somewhat formal, spirit. She spoke with the trace of a European accent and wore her hair pulled taut into a bun on the back of her head. I remember Rabbi Bernstein as thin, clean-shaven, and wearing black horn-rimmed spectacles. He always dressed in a black suit with an undistinguished necktie.

As Mrs. Bernstein entered the room bearing a snack for a hungry boy who was already apprehensive about the task he couldn't possibly complete, Rabbi Bernstein was impatient to start.

"Sarah, the boy isn't here to have dinner. He's here to learn Hebrew in six months that he should have been devoting himself to over the past six years."

He then lapsed into Yiddish for Mrs. Bernstein. In a few moments she was gone, shaking her head, never to return. Now it was Rabbi Bernstein and Master Lawson, one-on-one.

He didn't say it, but the attitude was more than clear. How could I have the *chutzpah*—the gall—to show up at this rabbi's house and expect to be ready for Bar Mitzvah in six months when it takes everyone else in the world year after year of study?

I had no doubt in my mind that I could do it. It wasn't long however, before a gathering fog of futility descended upon Rabbi Bernstein. A month passed, with no visible sign of improvement. Even I had become disenchanted with the whole idea. Another month passed. Rabbi Bernstein grew concerned, and I became disillusioned. Soon the rabbi was in a state of panic.

One Wednesday I walked into his study, and Rabbi Bernstein looked up with a trace of a smile on his lips—a treat he seldom afforded himself. With a burst of ingenuity, he shared a plan intended to save both our reputations, especially his.

"Stephen, there are only a little over two months left before your Bar Mitzvah. It should be apparent that if we continue as we have been going, there is no possibility that you can be prepared. I don't know what you've been doing in Temple all those years prior to moving here, but learning Hebrew wasn't included."

I laughed in embarrassment.

"Therefore, I have written your entire Bar Mitzvah phonetically underneath the Hebrew, to aid you in your studies."

Obviously, he was imploring me to stop studying and start memorizing.

After that, my studies progressed at a splendid rate. Soon I'd memorized the entire Hebrew portion, with a minimum of mispronunciation. And it seemed that Rabbi Bernstein was pleased with the patriarchal prerogative he had demonstrated.

For me, neither the pile of customary presents nor the idea of being the leading man in a "play" had spurred me on. It was simple, really; an entire family would respond to the Bar Mitzvah event. Aunts and uncles would come from out of town, and there'd be a festive mood. If I did well, they'd all congratulate my parents, who couldn't help but be proud of me. I wanted their love more than anything else in the world.

I had somehow come to believe that the constant fighting at home must be my fault. All my attempts at improving my daily behavior seemed to have failed. I was surrounded by vigilant suspicion and dislike. I needed this Bar Mitzvah. It was the big event, the success required to undo all the harm I thought I had caused.

On that day, my folks drove me to the Temple. Their serene behavior let me know that they were pleased to be a part of my big day. When I walked out to the pulpit with the rabbi and sat in a chair beside his, they smiled at me.

The Cantor sat on the other side of the ark that contained the Holy Scrolls, the Torah. As I looked into the congregation, I could see almost every seat taken. My Bar Mitzvah was made a part of a regular worship service, which accounted for the large attendance. On the first row, where members of my family sat, I saw huge smiles, waving hands, and other signals of encouragement.

Finally, my moment arrived. As I rose to accompany the rabbi to the ark to bring the Torah to the pulpit, my heart rejoiced. All the months of work had been worth it. Nothing could distract me. My parents showed their obvious pleasure. The day was turning out to be all I could have wished for.

The ark door opened, revealing the Torah, the embodiment of the Jewish faith. It contains the terms of the Jews' covenant with God. As the rabbi lifted the Torah from the ark and placed it in my arms, I looked at him. Rabbi Bernstein's entire existence was wrapped around and interwoven with the Torah and its teachings.

Suddenly, I felt like a fraud. Worse, I *knew* I was a fraud. I wanted to run. Oh, God, what had I done? If there really was a God, could he forgive me for what I had done and the mess I was in the midst of?

As we approached the pulpit, my family's encouraging expressions suddenly filled me with dismay. Though my parents knew I'd memorized, rather than learned, the Hebrew, they didn't seem to share the utter shame that I felt. My own despair contrasted oddly with the carnival atmosphere on the first row, the hand gestures that indicated, "Go get 'em, Tiger!" and "Do us proud, Son."

Relatives nudged each other with expectation. They were primed to share in my moment—a moment I recognized as a bizarre piece of play-acting.

The Torah was placed on the pulpit and opened. So much Hebrew, and I didn't know one letter from the next. Standing at my side with great bearing, the rabbi picked up a long silver pointer and placed it beside a symbol on the right-hand side of a line halfway down the scroll. He nodded his head for me to begin, much as a symphony conductor might communicate with his orchestra. I had no idea what I must do.

"Baruch es adonai," the rabbi suggested in a whisper. His lips never moved. I glanced at him. "Baruch es adonai," came the plea once more. Again, his lips did not move.

"Baruch es adonai," I began. "Baruch adonai hamvorach l'olam va-ed." Wonder of wonders, Rabbi Bernstein's pointer on the Torah was moving with the words I was muttering. I stopped thinking about fraud and concentrated on the business I had prepared for.

Words tumbled out of my mouth as the pointer moved faster. My fans on the front row were ecstatic. Now it wasn't enough to merely recite what I'd learned, but I began to ham it up, putting great emphasis on various words so as to produce a dramatic reading. The silver pointer could hardly keep up, and the rabbi gave a few quick glances in my direction. He must have thought I'd gone mad.

At last the ceremony ended. I accepted the congratulations of my parents and other relatives while the rabbi stood silently watching. I couldn't turn around and meet his eyes because I felt so guilty for what I had done.

I *had* been a fraud. But, on the other hand, what did it really matter? I had pleased my folks. Rabbi Bernstein, after all, had condoned it. Obviously, the end had justified the means.

That day a bad lesson in ethics got stored away for future use. In the years that followed, I learned to rationalize just about anything I chose to do on the basis of doing what I considered the situation demanded. Worst of all, I gave no thoughts of where such situational ethics or actions would eventually lead.

Chapter 5

Learning to Gamble

Dad went out of business a year later, and we moved to St. Louis. I enjoyed it there, though my school work started to decline. Life at home was hard, and never a day passed without turmoil. It didn't let up even when Dad became sick. He suffered a major stroke when I was fifteen, which left him unable to speak. He had to take speech lessons, and though years later I could discern no problems, Dad always felt his speech to be a second or two slower than his thought processes.

During the time Dad couldn't talk, it seemed that Mother yelled at him even louder. My heart would break as tears rolled down Dad's face, and I heard his sobs. At such times I realized, quite consciously, that I hated my mother. I loved her, too, strangely, but would have run away except that I couldn't desert Dad. Every time she exploded in bitterness, her anger infected everyone around her.

Soon it seemed best for me to live with an aunt in Louisville while Dad and Mother moved to Milwaukee, where he could be under the care of a specialist. I was relieved to escape our home situation, yet also tremendously sad. Dad was so sick that I wondered if I'd be saying good-bye to him for the last time.

I will forever remember the day they left for Milwaukee. I crossed the wet lawn after checking our empty apartment; Mother wanted to make sure they'd left nothing behind. It was a difficult moment, and I knew that saying good-bye to Dad would be emotional.

Suddenly, Mother sprang from the car and headed toward me with spiteful determination. She shouted about my ruining my shoes on the wet lawn and claimed I didn't show concern about anything. As usual, she tried to slap me. And, as usual, she used a right-hand lead, so I blocked it with little effort.

Because of that episode, one of my life's touching moments had been aborted. The good-bye was quick. I felt no compassion or love for either of them as they drove away.

In Louisville, I experienced the happiest days of my adolescence. At age fifteen, I found myself to be extremely popular and was continually in the middle of exciting happenings. After eighteen months there, I rejoined my parents in New York City.

Nothing had changed. I could feel the tension and unhappiness a mile away. We lived at the Bolivar, a residential hotel located on Central Park West at 83rd Street. We had one bedroom, one bath, and a tiny Pullman-type kitchen. I slept on a convertible sofa in the living room, and Mother cooked meals on a hot plate and a rotisserie portable grill.

Dad's health seemed greatly improved, but it gradually failed over the next ten years until his death. He held several jobs during that time but was often unemployed. He became a textile salesman, working on straight commissions for people he otherwise wouldn't have associated with. He had to carry his heavy samples from account to account. He wasn't given good accounts to service and continually struggled to establish new ones for himself. Physically, he couldn't handle it; he'd come home each night exhausted. During those times I learned how much I respected this man and, yes, how much I loved him. Until his death, he stayed optimistic about his future and held on to the sincere belief that things would be better. He never stopped trying.

To Mother's credit, she encouraged him to use the portable sun lamp each night so he'd present a prosperous, healthy appearance. Also, she'd iron his dress shirts and make sure they were perfectly wrinkle-free, even if she did complain loudly as she did them. Those memories still linger, and even now I much prefer to send everything out to be laundered—and not to see my wife, Harvey, standing behind an ironing board.

For years, Dad had made every effort to pay his creditors back. He had borrowed large sums of money to keep his former business afloat and couldn't imagine not honoring his debts. But, finally, he did go bankrupt. It seemed at that time that he had reached a poverty of soul as well. Lists were made of everything we could possibly need in the foreseeable future, everything from socks and underwear to bedding, furniture, radios, television sets, and expensive clothing. "If we're going to have the stigma of being bankrupt, we might as well go about it in the right way. If you're going to have the name you might as well play the game," Mom would say, enjoying this time of sudden affluence. Every credit card they owned and department store charge account they had were used, abused, and added to the list of creditors at the time Dad filed for bankruptcy.

Mother would take me shopping. "My son would like to see a suit in a banker's gray . . . Is this the best material you have? I don't like the feel of it at all!" she'd storm. "Yes, that's much better. . . . I understand it's in quite another price range than the other suit, but 'cheap *is* cheap.' When you know quality you can't settle for less," Mom would go on in expansive bellows of self-congratulation. In all honesty, I enjoyed the new clothes every bit as much as the jokes

Mother and I would secretly share in front of the salesperson who was writing up the order and charging it to our account. "Steve, I'm glad you listened to your mother," she would say. "It's more money, but when it comes to dressing my son right *money is no object*." I was a willing student in another lesson in situational ethics.

Other parts of our existence weren't nearly as pleasant. My mother and father went through ritualistic periods of guilt, concern, and remorse. They felt martyred by the neglect of friends who had faded away. Dad no longer wore a flower in his lapel. In the past, when we'd known prosperity, his money seemed to give him a certain aura. Now he looked and acted like any other short, uneducated, and unhappy man.

Dad attempted suicide when I was twenty-three by taking an overdose of sleeping pills and was saved through my administering mouth-to-mouth resuscitation until the doctor came. He was rushed to the hospital where, after a touch-and-go thirty-six hours, he pulled through. I found the bitter note he left for Mother and made sure she never saw it. In it, Dad claimed he'd taken the only way he knew to escape her. The overdose was her fault as much as if she had pulled the trigger of a gun, he wrote. As life continued with little tranquility or peace, I often felt I had done Dad a disservice by reviving him that evening.

It was during this period that two major beginnings took place in my life: gambling, and the horrible feelings of loneliness that would recur at significant points in my life.

To assuage those episodes of shattering desolation, I often attended services at the Temple. But religion didn't satisfy the emptiness. I even attempted to read the Bible—the Old Testament, of course, since I didn't know anyone who owned a New Testament. Somehow I sensed a spiritual void. I started at the beginning and read most of Genesis before putting the book down as too unbelievable. I continued life on my own . . . and alone.

By this time I was a student at New York University. My life suffered even more in comparison to that of some of my friends. Peter continually bought expensive clothes; Ronnie purchased a new car; David spent summers at the Lido Beach Hotel; and Norm was able to save his money and use it however he wished. Not so for me. I perceived that I was part of a caste system in which things could not possibly improve.

Everyone I knew had much the same things in common. They ate Chinese food on Sundays, played gin rummy at the club, and loved to bet on a ball game. Not only that, everyone, but *everyone* had a bookmaker.

If you didn't have your own bookmaker but attended a game at Madison Square Garden, it didn't matter, since there were more bookmakers in The Garden than paying fans, it seemed. The truth is, most of my friends enjoyed the status of having a personal bookmaker. With this dubious honor came the recognition that someone believed in you enough to provide a line of credit that no bank, certainly, would extend.

Since I wasn't able to bet enough to have my own account, for many years I bet through others. That posed no restriction, since people welcomed additional action on their accounts. Thus they appeared to be bigger bettors than they actually were—a good impression to give a bookmaker. We all learned how to make good impressions—that is to say, puffed-up ones. This became a way of life.

I was in high school when I placed my first bet on the N.I.T. basketball finals. I bet ten dollars and watched the game with my heart in my mouth, knowing full well I'd have a hard time coming up with ten dollars if I lost.

Fortunately (or so I thought back then), I won that first bet. When I received my ten-dollar winnings the next week I experienced the rush of "making it big." I could anticipate more of this easy money, since it seemed effortless to pick more winners than losers. Now I could do as much as the next guy, and be as big a sport as my friends were. Betting offered me a way out of my circumstances. The bet itself was a thrill, since it brought excitement into an otherwise dull existence. You see, all the money I made at various jobs went to my parents, except for a few dollars I kept for car fare and meals.

I could never buy anything tangible with my winnings, of course, since my folks would be sure to question the source of my money. But I could spend the money on myself and believe I was more like other people—a person of means.

My friend David gave me some helpful tips on conducting myself as a bettor. "The first thing you did wrong when you won that ten dollars was to stop betting. You let the bookie off the hook."

"What do you mean?" I queried. "I won ten dollars, and he paid me."

"That's what I mean. You have no betting mentality. When you were ahead ten dollars, you should have made two other ten-dollar bets. You know that your chances of winning both are much greater than your losing both—aren't they?"

I thought a minute. "Of course."

"Okay then. If you win both, you're up thirty dollars and can sock him a bet—maybe twenty dollars or so. If you split your bet, nothing has been lost, and if you lose both, it's no big deal. After all, you were up ten dollars already, so you'd be only a ten-dollar winning bet away from being even again."

I could see that David was correct. He had also pointed out to me that I had a loser's mentality, a guy who would be grateful for crumbs instead of the sort who'd seize opportunity by the throat and take full advantage.

I concluded that it was the difference between two types of people: those who hadn't experienced all the negatives of life and therefore could still afford to go about living in a rational, meaningful way . . . and me.

—◆—

The next several weeks produced the sort of success I could only have dreamed of. I won seventy dollars, ninety-five dollars, ninety dollars . . . and since I couldn't buy anything tangible, I was able to date. When David and I double-dated, taking the girls out to dinner, I appeared a man of means, as did my friends. I was tasting the good life, and couldn't imagine ever having a losing week. The fact is, I did lose, and often. Later, I started diverting my paycheck from my folks, offering various excuses. Our relationship grew worse.

I often lied to them, saying that I was to have dinner at a friend's house, when in fact I was taking a date to one of New York's finest restaurants. Other times, I was at Yonkers Raceway when I had told them I was somewhere else. For the most part, my lies were accepted without question. When they did question what I said, I stayed one step ahead of them, arranging alibis and supporting lies from my friends.

My new life concept had taken firm root. Everything my parents had taught me, everything my friends were showing me, proved the importance of having spendable money in order to make the right impressions. I would look for the best risk/reward ratio. I learned more about the fine points of situational ethics and the best ways to manipulate others through rationalization of conduct.

Like any other person subject to an addiction, I was the last to know or even suspect what was happening. I just knew that betting offered me a chance to enjoy life, and I was confident that I could win much more than I'd lose. It became easy to rationalize any losses as merely bad luck.

My betting started when I was in high school and continued uninterrupted until I was forty-one. That self-deceived mental posture permeated every area of my life and led to my downfall.

Eventually, betting cost me almost everything I had. Some of my bets were bigger than I would ever care to admit. Like many other men addicted to gambling, I grew reckless—with my name, my business, my personal integrity, and, eventually, even with my wife and child.

Chapter 6

Falling in Love

Harvey was the first girl I ever dated who was neither Jewish nor wealthy. For twenty-seven years I figured if I limited my dating to those who were Jewish *and* had money, I would decrease my chances of marrying some poor Gentile. About an hour before we met, I learned that Harvey was Episcopalian.

"That's one rung under Roman Catholic, isn't it?" I asked my friend David.

"I have no idea," he replied, "but they shake hands when they're introduced to you. Can you imagine that? I mean, can you picture a Jewish girl saying, 'It's very nice to meet you' and shaking hands?"

We considered that quite humorous. We dressed British and thought Yiddish, and since we were ignorant we didn't consider ourselves bigoted.

It was mid-season for the major sports teams. We lived in the East so we could calculate our winnings from game to game before betting on events about to start on the West Coast. It had been a normal Sunday afternoon, with David and me monitoring our various bets and ball games. The bookmaker's office would be open until eight. Our tab was carried from Tuesday to the following Monday, and by Sunday we were betting on a per-game basis. If we were losing, we used Sunday to break even, or we verified that we were ahead. If ahead, we rationalized that we were betting with their money, so by "laying it in" we could chance to make a lot of money without risk.

By seven that evening we had placed our last bets. David turned off the television set. Peter, an old friend since childhood days, stood idly by. He'd come to watch the games with us but seldom placed a bet. David and I dished out quite a bit of ridicule to Peter, whose conservative attitude toward betting afforded us little in common.

We'd had a good week, and David felt pleased. "Time for Chinese food," he announced briskly. "As a matter of fact, rather than go alone, let's call up a few beautiful girls and ask them to join us."

"Terrific idea, David, let's do it," I agreed, smiling broadly.

Peter fell right into our ploy. "Hey! All right! Who do you guys have in mind?"

David looked as though Peter were crazy. "Come on, Peter, you're the ladies' man. You always talk about the fabulous girls you meet in the advertising business. If you're not full of baloney, make a phone call. You have enough names to share!"

Peter knew he was trapped. We never supposed that he was the ladies' man he professed to be, but he had been bragging, and it was time to produce. Actually, we didn't think he would come through.

"There are two girls—roommates—who live near here," he said. "I dated the one from Atlanta who moved up here to get into show business. I selected her to be our national Miss Man-Tan—"

"I remember that product. It was taken off the market. She isn't still yellow, is she, Peter? We wouldn't want to be embarrassed by being seen with her on the street," David teased.

"Aw, come on, guys," he responded, "these two *shiksas* are beautiful and real society types. Are you interested or not?"

"Sure we're interested. Give them a call," I replied.

When Peter got off the phone with some half-baked excuse about striking out, David and I refused to take it lying down. Since they lived close by we'd go to their apartment, uninvited, and see for ourselves what Peter referred to as being beautiful and from real society.

The doorman stopped us, asked us who we were and who we wanted to see. New Yorkers are raised on such challenges as that, so it presented little trouble for us. "Miss Reinhard and Miss Doherty are expecting us. That's the ninth floor, isn't it? Thank you!"

We were past him in a flash and into the elevator, and within moments were inside with the girls, who were kindly but firmly admonishing Peter for arriving uninvited. We sided with the girls, in a chorus of criticism, telling them they were absolutely correct and that Peter had insisted on bringing us to see them. Peter wasn't considerate of them at all, we said with feigned annoyance.

Soon Peter, filled with frustration and righteous indignation, made a grandstand move. "Well, if that's the way you feel, I'll leave right now. Come on guys, let's go."

"Peter, why don't you go ahead, and we'll give you a call tomorrow," we chorused.

"The girls are upset, and as long as we interrupted them anyhow, we're going to take them out for dinner someplace in the neighborhood so we can say we're sorry." I offered up my most sincere-looking expression. Exit, Peter. Enter, romance.

Peter wasn't wrong. These girls really were beautiful, especially the blond. At the restaurant our conversation raced along. It was wonderful being with this girl named Harvey.

By dessert, I could contain myself no longer. As Harvey offered me cream for my coffee, I blurted, "No, thanks, but I do take two sugars, and I wish you'd try to remember that because I have a feeling you'll be doing it the rest of your life."

Harvey looked at me incredulously. Her mother had told her that New Yorkers were prone to be crazy, and now she'd met one for sure.

"I beg your pardon," she said. David was right; no Jewish girl would have said, "I beg your pardon."

"Listen, Harvey, I'm not crazy," I began. "I'm twenty-seven and not a guy who falls in love every time he goes out. In fact, I don't think I've dated the same girl twice in a row. But somehow, I know we're going to be married. So as soon as we can get through asking about backgrounds and making small talk we can probably start enjoying a pretty decent relationship."

In years to come, Harvey would relate that she thought I was the craziest person she'd ever met, but found me attractive anyway. She says she felt secure with me, and that I had the ability to be a good friend. My previous track record of dishonorable intentions with women indicated otherwise but, despite that, Harvey and I became immediate and irrevocable best friends. Her manner advertised her loyalty.

As Harvey was to write about that first meeting:

Enter Stephen. He was so nice . . . almost too nice, and too clean-cut, but he had fabulous personality, certainly not dull. I enjoyed being with him. I had always been attracted to dark, mysterious, and, frequently, Semitic-looking men. But he was fair-skinned, blue-eyed with light brown—almost blond—hair, and the sweetest face I'd ever seen.

There we were, on that first date, standing at P.J. Clark's waiting for a table and holding hands, and I was thinking: He is the nicest man I have ever met.

By the next day, I was telling myself that it wasn't logical to suppose I'd fallen in love with this girl after only three hours the night before. But my thoughts centered around her. Our next date was on her birthday, that Saturday evening. I bought her a simple but beautiful gold pin with rose-colored pearls. It had been a good betting week, and I had the cash; even so, my friends thought I was nuts. "You don't spend fifty dollars on some *shiksa* you've seen only once!" I invited them to dinner so they could meet Harvey. She was incredibly beautiful and delightful, and she won everyone's heart, especially mine. She still wears the pin.

Although Harvey had specific career goals in mind, her feelings were fast becoming as strong as mine. She would write:

It was disarming, and I was totally unprepared for that turn of events. I had come to New York for stardom, not a husband.

Dad took Harvey to his heart immediately. He placed his arm around her and demanded a kiss on his cheek, saying, "We have generations of beautiful women in our family! My father married a beautiful woman, I married a beautiful woman, and it's incumbent on my son also to marry a beautiful woman."

Mother had more of a problem about my dating Harvey than Dad seemed to have. First, Harvey wasn't Jewish. Second, she was in show business. Besides, I couldn't afford to take care of myself, much less a wife. To Mother, who wasn't exactly my biggest fan, the thought of someone having confidence in me and loving me was preposterous. She attempted to negate the relationship, using typically nonsubtle means.

"Steve, please tell Harvey not to wear false eyelashes so early in the morning. If she *must* wear them, she should find some that aren't so long."

"Why don't you tell her yourself," I answered curtly, all the while praying for clemency.

Mother started with compliments, telling Harvey she was a beautiful girl, with gorgeous skin and big blue eyes, but that she *did* have one suggestion, if Harvey didn't mind . . .

"Of course, Mrs. Lawson."

"Well, dear, it's those eyelashes. It's a pity for you to wear something so obviously made-up," Mother commented. "They might be all right in the evening if you have a formal affair to attend but, otherwise, it's a case of being too overdressed. Why don't you go into the bathroom and take them off so I can see how you look without them?"

Harvey looked a little mystified, but determined. "Mrs. Lawson," she replied, "Most people wouldn't have the courage to make such a suggestion, and I appreciate your caring enough about me to bring it up. The main problem, though, is that these *are* my eyelashes. For better or worse, they go where I go."

Mother was flabbergasted . . . and bested. From then on, she made sure to point out to everyone that the lashes were Harvey's own—and that they were *fabulous!*

Harvey and I saw each other steadily, over the objections and concern of both her mother and her brother-in-law. It was bad enough that I was Jewish, he told her, but who ever heard of a Jew without money? "He's going with you for one reason," he warned her. "He'll get what he can, then dump you for a Jewish girl."

Even then, Harvey had insight into both our lives:

Stephen was even more goal-oriented than I was, and our needs complemented one another's. Mother visualized me becoming somebody, and Stephen's mother told him he would never be anybody. Mother pushed me to be a success; Stephen's threw a curse on him by saying he'd end up a failure. We both had our eyes fixed on a goal; we both needed to prove our worthiness. We were on our way and knew we could make it with each other's support. What a great team we were!

Yes, Harvey might be sugar, spice, and everything nice, but I learned she could handle herself under pressure and unfair tactics, too. It was done with a smile, and she remained a lady. However, her walk was the tip-off. It was the most determined walk I had ever seen—feminine, but with purpose. She didn't wander from point A to point B. She strode there with vigor. That same spirit carried over into every facet of her life. It would be a greater benefit in our life together than either of us could foresee.

Chapter 7

Love and Marriage

My being Jewish put no more strain on our growing relationship than did Harvey's non-Jewishness. We agreed that the only problem was that perceived by others. Religion meant almost nothing to us, so we decided to rear our children as Jews if we lived in New York, since everyone I knew was Jewish. Harvey thought she should assimilate so that our children would have no ethnic disadvantages.

If we settled in the South, however, we'd rear our children as Episcopalians. I readily agreed to that since I didn't much care one way or the other. Also, I assumed it was a non-risk compromise in that we'd live in New York, anyway.

Dad died during this time, and each afternoon for the next year I'd go to Temple and say "Kaddish," the mourner's prayer, in respect for his memory. This ritual had no effect on Harvey's and my relationship, and I continued secure in the belief that religion would never become an issue in our marriage.

As the months continued, however, Harvey suffered recurrent bouts of bronchitis, often severe enough to make her spend nights sitting up in bed to enable her to breathe. Her physician advised that cold air, smoking, and New York air pollution would lead to emphysema someday. The

situation caused us enough concern to warrant consideration of a move to Atlanta.

There was nothing to hold us in New York except for the
city's excitement and challenge. I could earn the same insurance commissions in Atlanta as in New York, I imagined, and perhaps even more. Harvey, typically, hated to turn
her back on professional success. After all, she'd disciplined
herself for years and longed to fulfill those personal goals.

Soon I found myself flying to Atlanta to attend our an-
nouncement party, a lovely gathering arranged by Marjory,
Harvey's mother. Harvey's friends were nice and seemed
genuinely interested in this Yankee she had brought South.
It was springtime in Atlanta—everything in full bloom—
and I fell in love with the area in no time.

The change in scene, though, brought some realizations
to me. For the first time since I'd met Harvey, the religion
issue made me uneasy. How could I get married in a
church? I'd never knelt to pray. And they'd probably mention Jesus Christ throughout the service, which would give
Mother apoplexy as she sat in the pew.

Mother was no more religious than I. Blonde and a petite
five-foot-one, my blue-eyed mother didn't look a bit Jewish.
Yet we *were* Jewish, and if we strayed far from our heritage
we felt uncomfortable. The bond far exceeds common worship and goes deep into cultural areas such as food, humor,
homeland, types of business, history, and perceptions. All
my instincts made me feel wary about marriage in a church,
just as I knew Mother's did. Dad might even turn in his
grave as we said our "I do's."

At this point Harvey reminded me of our early agreement concerning religion. *I'm going to have to do the changing!* I thought. *What a lousy deal I made. I never dreamed we'd
live in Georgia—that's the Deep South!*

But I had found a life's partner in Harvey. Nothing
would prevent our marriage. I'd become Chinese if that's

what it took for me to have her as my wife. I'd become Southern *and* Episcopalian.

Though it was never spoken by either of us, an agreement was made not to tell people I was Jewish. I didn't look the part, so why subject myself even to unintentional anti-Semitism? If people asked, I'd say we belonged to All Saints, the Episcopal church where we were married. Thus we founded our marriage on a white lie and considered the situational ethics totally unimportant.

Four months later, Harvey resigned her job as a dancer and departed for Atlanta to give attention to wedding preparations. I'd join her a week prior to the wedding for last-minute parties and the practical work of finding an apartment, a car, and a job. Soon my departure date arrived, and I kissed Mother good-bye. She had gone from rage to relative docility by now; the idea of my being married in a church and not the Temple had made life miserable at home ever since she found out.

"Mother, why are you making such a big deal out of this?" I'd argued. "You're an atheist, anyway."

"That may be true," she screamed, "But I'm a Jewish atheist and don't you ever forget it!"

But she would join us to host the rehearsal dinner and, yes, even attend the wedding.

Thus I left behind my old life.

Harvey was a beautiful bride. I'd seen her in many shows, commercials, and other appearances, but our wedding far exceeded any of her other performances. I was a proud groom! As she stood at the back of the church, waiting for the music to begin, I glanced at Mother, sitting in the front pew. She looked old and lonely, sitting there without Dad. I felt the sting of regret that he couldn't share this day with me. Mother's face mirrored the hard life she'd experienced, and for a moment my heart went out to her. It wasn't that I hadn't tried to express my love to her in the past, but she had never stopped fighting long enough to hear. There were always old fights to be rehashed and new battles to be waged. Mother taught me a lot about hating. She had demonstrated that hatred could be a great motivator. She herself was unable to forgive and prided herself that she never forgot. Nevertheless, in that instant on my wedding day I loved her very much and crossed to where she sat and kissed her on the cheek.

Without understanding what I'd done, I had *forgiven* for the first time in my life. I forgave all things past and wiped the slate clean. It was marvelous. Unfortunately, that forgiveness came from my own effort rather than the power of God's love. It wasn't long, therefore, in the heat of conflict, that I took my forgiveness back.

Harvey and I were not nervous as we said our vows. The altar kneeling was not as bad as I'd imagined, and Jesus' name was not mentioned too often. The end of the ceremony was exactly like that of a Jewish wedding: money was given to the priest in a plain white envelope to express gratitude for a lovely ceremony.

Driving toward our honeymoon at Sea Island, Georgia, we experienced a strange—and to Harvey, a significant—happening. As we traveled down the country road that approached our hotel, three white doves flew across the road and narrowly missed our windshield.

Harvey was ecstatic. While it had no significance to me, Harvey knew beyond doubt that we'd witnessed an omen of good fortune. She mentioned that the doves represented the Trinity, which was God the Father, God the Son, and

God the Holy Spirit. She told me that God used a dove to impart the Holy Spirit to Jesus.

I was totally uninterested. Such conversation was wasted on a Jewish boy from New York. Some days later, however, when we'd returned from our seaside honeymoon and moved into our eighth-floor apartment, there came a sign with meaning for *me*.

It was the morning after our arrival, and I was savoring every moment of it. Until this time, home to me had been merely a house, a place to be avoided because it hurt too much to be there. But I truly had a home now, a place where I could be sheltered from the world's turmoil, a safe harbor. To most men, home means a woman, too—his mother when he's young, and his wife when he's an adult. Across the table from me was the pivotal part of my home—Harvey. Over our coffee we looked out the open window at the beautiful view. There was a delightful breeze playing around us, and minutes earlier the rain had stopped. Now the sun broke through.

"Look, a rainbow!" we said together, looking into the distance at the most vivid arc I'd ever seen. The radiant colors were perfectly displayed.

At first, looking into the distance, we missed what was happening several inches from where we stood. Then we saw it . . . the rainbow's end, lodged in *our* window sill. The end of the rainbow! Here it was!

Like children, we stretched forth our hands and delighted to see the colors wash over our skin. For long moments we experienced the pure magic of this mystical event, something we would always remember.

"Harvey, if this is the end of the rainbow, where's the pot of gold?" I asked.

We looked at each other, now husband and wife, and smiled in agreement. The pot of gold was a myth, after all.

Chapter 8

Selling the Sizzle

The life insurance business wasn't going too well for me in those early days of our marriage. I hadn't wanted Harvey to work outside our home; my male ego proclaimed loudly that I should supply all her needs. But our not being able to meet the rent on time every month dictated that she help out. Harvey worked for several years until I went into business for myself.

While I starved in the insurance business, the St. Louis Hawks professional basketball team moved to Atlanta. When the team had been in town for a week, I approached the general manager about a job.

I began serving as statistician, working for press tickets, free game passes for Harvey, and ten dollars per game. I thought I'd died and gone to heaven. Within months, the general manager gave me a full-time position: director of sales. I enjoyed this job. It was a lot of fun to mention my position at cocktail parties. It certainly beat saying you sold insurance and watching people walk away. My popularity picked up considerably.

After two great years with the Hawks, I decided to form my own real estate investment firm. A close friend had left one of Atlanta's prestigious legal firms to open his own real estate investment and development enterprise, which prospered beautifully. He accepted the role of mentor in my commercial future. At first the thought of starting my own firm was a passing whim. But why not? I might not be a genius, but I hadn't met any since moving to Atlanta anyway. I was amazed at some of the people I saw who were prospering here, people who I knew would never make it in New York. It was a situation fit for an old gambler.

I instinctively knew what produced success. Impressions. Money. Thinking one step ahead of one's clients. The boy who had memorized the Bar Mitzvah ceremony could create investment sales pitches with far less difficulty.

I knew I could soon learn the basics of the business; I also knew that land prices in Atlanta were increasing at an unbelievable rate. Unquestionably, real estate ventures didn't *lose* money, ever. The issue that separated one deal from another was merely the size of the profit.

My talent consisted of selling the sizzle, not the steak. I sold "capital appreciation" and "interest write-offs" instead of real estate. It centered upon coaxing, cajoling, enticing, weaving stories, mentioning how few units were left . . . motivating buyers to quick decisions. It involved "sell-back provisions" that afforded buyers a false feeling of security and created a general smoke-blowing sort of existence I'd almost come to believe myself.

I did not consider myself unethical or greedy. I never sold my own property to any investment group I sponsored, and I never made a secret profit. All my investors knew I bought several units of ownership myself, which meant I'd certainly want to sell the property for as much as possible. Further, I made no additional commissions when the property eventually sold.

I considered myself one of the most reputable guys in town. A little puffing here and fudging there wouldn't affect anything, as long as my investors profited in the long run. Only a jerk would say that the ends didn't justify the means.

Large commissions began to roll in. I'd never made money so easily. It was unbelievable! Harvey and I celebrated our fifth anniversary by taking a trip to the North Carolina mountains, a memorable trip because my confidence had started to build. I didn't need to feel a secret rush of envy when I looked at successful people. Now they could envy me!

I hadn't forgotten, however, those who said I'd never make it, and that I'd never amount to anything—including my mother, who topped the list. Long ago I'd recognized the positive uses of such negative influences.

Many people work hard for the things that money can buy: vacations, automobiles, houses, and the like. My motivations were much more base. Any material success I ever realized—and that was considerable—arrived in direct proportion to my ability to hate. It was that hatred—simmering, controlled, and disguised—that provided the motivation and strength to work as hard as was necessary to accomplish success.

And the success felt wonderful, because it vindicated Harvey's decision to marry me. She believed in me before anyone else did, and I intended her to share in my success in a most deserved fashion. The things I gave her—the beautiful home, antiques, the pleasure of designer dresses and jewelry, fine restaurants, trips, a full-length mink coat—offered tangible proof that I was no loser. Harvey was proud of me, and I took considerable pride in knowing that. Life built on a basis of performance is all right as long as you are able to perform. I could—and would continue to.

Yes, success had a price tag. I was willing to pay the tariff. I was ready, determined, and dedicated. Without realizing it, I'd called on all the help this world could afford.

Satan answered, and I became a working partner with the demons of manipulation and deception. What a team we made!

Chapter 9

Love and Money

Closing followed closing, and I headed for more success than I'd ever dreamed of attaining. Harvey no longer had to work. Instead, we could take trips to Bermuda and other lovely places, buying beautiful clothes before and during each journey. Two new Mercedes-Benz automobiles ornamented our driveway. We often attended the Florida racetracks to watch our thoroughbreds run. We ate in the very best restaurants, and often. Our lives were changing drastically, Harvey's as much as mine. As she described at that time:

Stephen was so sure of himself, confident, bright, and tenacious. I knew I could trust him with my very life. I loved to work with him on any project, but I excelled at being Mrs. Stephen P. Lawson. President or Chairman always came after my name where it appeared in newspaper captions that documented our life.

I was a leader in several of the art organizations in town, receiving a great deal of attention and recognition for my capabilities. I was a tireless worker in the community, which might be expected of the youngest president of a major arts organization. I was pictured with the Mayor and the Governor for my efforts as a creative fund raiser. I presented silver cups at horse shows and received awards and plaques for my efforts and achievements.

While I was a star in the volunteer community, Stephen attained success as one of the five largest privately owned real estate investment firms in Atlanta. We were a sought-after couple—on the go seven days a week, the phones constantly ringing. I kept saying yes to volunteer commitments because these tasks provided me solid feelings of worthiness and power. My decisions meant something. I attained a high profile in the volunteer community.

The thing that separated me from others in the Atlanta real-estate syndication market was that I majored in people, not land. "You know, Bob," I'd say, "a fringe benefit of my business is that I meet so many people, including *some* I really like. I sure would like the girls to have an opportunity to meet one another, and I was thinking, I have four tickets to the basketball game this Thursday evening. Why don't we all plan to go? Let's get a bite to eat at the Omni Club beforehand."

I operated from a kind of cunning self-deception. Knowing that all of us want to be loved, I resolved to "love" my clients and shower them with thoughtfulness and generosity. Actually, it wasn't love at all but a new form of my old manipulative habits, one so subtle that even I didn't recognize it.

Sometimes Harvey and I went out sixteen evenings straight, entertaining potential investors. Not all invested with my firm, of course, but ninety percent did.

What's more, these investors referred me to others. Referrals, by and large, come from people who consider you a friend, and I was accumulating more "friends" than anyone else in town.

My attorneys were friends, too—or at least one of them was. He had opened his own firm, specializing in criminal law, several years before. Recently he had taken a partner. I recall a meeting at Hilton Head Island to discuss their representing me in the formation of land syndications.

They acknowledged knowing nothing about real estate but agreed to learn and represent me because of the sizable fees I'd generate.

Life was a piece of cake, and everything Mother had told me about making money was true: "Remember, Steve, you're nothing without money. A buck is your best friend." In truth, Mother never taught me the value of a dollar; she taught me the value of one hundred thousand dollars.

And she appeared to be right. Harvey and I were becoming more and more in demand. I was successful enough that people were laughing harder at my stories. Even my brother-in-law invested with the kid brother who was taking the world by storm down there in Atlanta.

Marjory, my mother-in-law, claimed I was a genius. I secretly admired her discernment. My office had to be enlarged in order to house a person of my intelligence, kindness, and shrinking humility. Class A personalities asked for my opinions about things.

One Monday morning my secretary called to say she'd be late, and I found myself alone, contemplating a conversation Harvey and I had had the evening before.

"Stephen, I have a funny feeling, and it's important that we discuss it."

"Of course, Honey. What is it?"

"There's no one in the world happier about your—our—success than I am. I enjoy being the wife of a man who's successful, and I love being able to do all the things we dreamed of doing, but . . ."

"But what?"

"Well, the truth is, something is missing."

"What do you mean?"

"I don't know . . . remember when you worked at the Hawks' office and we'd go down after dinner, and I'd help you with a lot of things because you didn't have a secretary?"

"Yeah, I sure do. We were both working, and our biggest project was paying off the Standard Oil bill so they'd return our credit card."

Harvey laughed a little at the recollection. "Honey, that's what I mean when I said something is missing. Somehow we don't have the same satisfaction we seemed to have back then."

Harvey's comments didn't disturb me; they left me more curious than anything else. Our relationship was as good as ever. True, we worked very hard, but only so we could enjoy things together.

If I had been honest, though, I would have told Harvey that I also felt something was missing. Despite the money I was making, I still couldn't seem to buy the respect of those I most wanted to impress—the ones with negative predetermined opinions of me—some family members, several friends in New York and, of course, my mother.

I worked so hard to show them they were wrong about me but still hadn't obtained the thrill to which I felt entitled. Money wasn't turning out to be the great reward I had expected.

Each month I sent my mother four hundred dollars to help meet her monthly obligations, and the only satisfaction it gave me was to see her signature on the cashed checks. Actually, she never needed the money as much as I needed to send it. I needed her to see how well I was doing and how wrong she had been about me. It was my way of rubbing her nose in it on a thirty-day basis.

But that was not my main problem. I knew that I was a fraud, that I was not the financial mind I purported to be in the sales pitches I was forever giving. Actually, I was no smarter than when I had struggled in the insurance business; I was merely more calculating and brazen.

I was a real gunslinger, and no one seemed to see it but me. I also felt somewhat awkward about the money I was making. Based on the effort expended, I had to be earning more money per ounce of effort than anyone else in the world.

I couldn't philosophize long that day, as I pondered my conversation with Harvey and faced momentarily my own moral discomforts. I had been rich and I had been poor, and as a comedian once said, "Rich is better."

There was a bigger problem that needed my attention at that time. I'd sponsored an investment earlier and collected all the monies required for closing by getting it fully subscribed. The problem was, I had to pay my bookmaker for my accumulated gambling losses. So I took money from the limited partnership account.

At first I took only the amount of the commission I was due to earn. Advancing commissions prior to the closing was wrong enough, but I did not stop there. Later I took substantially more. I was raised on a New York code of ethics that was true everywhere: either pay your bookie on time or assume, most correctly, that you had wished you had. When closing time arrived, I lacked funds needed to complete the property purchase. Of course I planned to pay it all back when my luck changed next week.

What could I do? Obviously I must obtain an extension until I was able to close. I bought an extra thirty days by taking another five thousand dollars from the limited partnership account.

In all, I obtained three extensions, but was unable to negotiate a fourth. How could I get out of this one?

"Right, Sam,*" I lied to an investor, "we had the closing yesterday, and I think there's already someone interested in buying this property from us. The thing is, we need to hold it for six months to qualify for the capital gains treatment . . . "

Alone in my air-conditioned office, I began to sweat with the effort it took to keep my voice casual, neither hurried nor loud, while I maneuvered myself out of a dangerously tight corner with an investor who wouldn't get off the phone.

"How much is he talking about? Well, I'm looking at getting our original investment back with about a 40 percent profit! That's 80 percent, if you figure it on an annual basis . . . That's right, Sam, we could have held it longer but, as Dad used to say, 'You can't go broke taking a profit' . . . "

At last he hung up. I mopped the sweat off my face and told my heart to stop pounding. I didn't have their money, and they didn't have an investment. I'd just sold Sam a bunch of hot air but had bought myself some time. Given six months, I'd get out of this mess. Of course, had I told Sam the truth, I could have been put out of business. I was smart enough to know that my conduct was criminal. I knew I had to come up with some gambling winnings or earn some new commissions. Either way, I kept telling myself, "No problem."

Within six months I accomplished what I'd set out to do. Each investor received back his original investment plus a forty percent cash profit, which came directly from my pocket.

I considered the matter closed—expensively closed, but closed. For the first time in over eight months I was able to take a deep breath without trembling.

I knew gambling had me in its hold, and I wanted to stop, or at least cut back. Unfortunately, I'd see bargains I couldn't pass up without a heavy bet. By now, my bookmaker was far ahead of me. I had to make substantial bets if I was to have any prospect of getting my money back. Now I was betting just to break even.

Harvey had become aware that I was betting, but she had no idea of the amounts involved. We had arguments from time to time, when she caught me red-handed—and red-faced—talking to my bookmaker on the telephone.

I had developed an inexhaustible tolerance for a dark and secretive way of life. Winnings could never change my life. I had reached a point where my wants and desires couldn't keep pace with my earning capacity. When I lost, I had to rendezvous with the bookmaker to pay off my debts. Every expression and word out of his mouth mocked me. Drawing large sums of cash out of the bank made me feel dirty and uneasy. I had to endure the cute remarks from a bank teller who asked if I were paying a kidnapper later in the day.

But, in spite of all this, I would tell Harvey I had to leave the house for a few minutes to get a newspaper or to buy something at the store—so that I could call the bookie from a phone booth. The line could be busy for twenty minutes at a time, and in the winter the temperature might be twenty degrees with a wind chill factor of minus three. But I kept dialing until the line was free. I returned home and wouldn't leave the television set. Weekends revolved around the games. Sometimes I was euphoric, but most of the time my feelings were cluttered junctions of fury, dismay, anger, and frustration. At all times I attempted to conceal my life. Gambling was morbid compulsion—something I would never have let my worst enemy do to me.

Nothing could make me stop. Though I loved Harvey more than anything else in the world, that love couldn't force me to stop. Betting continued. Losing continued. Never did I stop to realize that I was addicted, and the stakes were higher than I could imagine: Harvey, our marriage, our way of life.

Meanwhile, certain investors proved helpful in the area of cash flow. This group invested with me each time I had an offering. Since many closings were so far in the future, I sold them on the idea that it was silly to have all their savings sitting in credit unions earning a modest interest. I offered these investors an opportunity to pool their money with others in Certificates of Deposit I was purchasing at a much higher yield. Naturally, that certain group decided to take advantage of such a good idea. But there were no Certificates of Deposit, nor would there ever be.

They're getting the interest they seek, I rationalized. *I'll pay it out of my commissions. Since they invest with me so regularly anyway, I'm doing no more than advancing myself what would be future commissions.*

The only problem with this smooth scheme was that my actions were morally wrong. And, as I would eventually find out, I would be found criminally accountable also.

Chapter 10

The Approaching Storm

Harvey and I approached 1974 from two distinctly different perspectives. For me, there was the relief of knowing I'd weathered the past year and all its problems. Not only had I pulled my business out of its troubles, but I'd earned more than half a million dollars and expected the coming year to be even better. (To put that 1972 earnings in better perspective, the most prestigeous estate in Atlanta sold for $300,000. That same residence in 1992 sells for 3.5 million.)

Also, I was cleaning up my act somewhat. I had cut way back on my betting and had hired a CPA firm to put my books in order and closely monitor me in the future by setting up accounts I couldn't invade. I'd made a full disclosure of my past year's dealings and believed they'd provide a good check on my activities.

I knew I'd walked into the lion's den the year before and was lucky I'd come out alive. I wouldn't have that happen again. Next time I might not survive!

Harvey, meanwhile, expected our first child in late January. It had been a wonderful pregnancy, and we looked forward to becoming parents. We had waited eight years to start a family, and it seemed our timing was perfect. Harvey expressed it this way:

I wanted to slow down long enough to have a family, and while I was pregnant my first feelings of fear surfaced. We had every-thing . . . all the money anyone could use, a beautiful home, cars, clothes, jewelry, and the invitation I had worked so hard to attain. I was invited into the Junior League.

I was on a cloud for a while, but then that feeling of "is this all there is?" became prominent. I said it to Stephen more than once and found myself crying for several days. We had worked so hard to achieve all this, but now that I was slowing down and had time for reflection, it didn't look so great. Stephen assured me my feelings were just hormonal.

Our baby arrived on the fifth of February. We called our new son Blake. At home, our happiness scale peaked when Blake came into our lives. At work, the curve began to nose dive. My troubles began to take shape on April 5, 1974, with a phone call from my accountants. I'd heeded their advice and made several changes in my business, one area being that of my legal representation.

"I know you want to give those fellows your business," my accountants said, "but they can get you into more trouble than you dream. We represent a lot of men in your industry and are familiar with the sort of legal work you require. You've simply got to retain attorneys who special-ize in securities."

Previously, one of the accountants phoned to warn me to be sure to have my attorneys file the limited partnership paperwork concerning my 1973 closings by April 1, 1974. "Steve, did you have them file with the state securities office?"

"Of course. You reminded me months ago, and I've reminded them several times. They assured me they'd take care of it."

"That's good, because it's quite a problem if they don't. Let's get a photostat of those documents from their files."

At that point, we learned that the prepared documents never had been filed with the state. Georgia securities laws had changed, meanwhile, and there was no saving clause that would allow a late filing. When my former attorneys belatedly attempted to file, the answer was no.

The office of my former attorneys was in the same building as my office. We called a meeting that included my accountants and new attorneys, with the intent to coordinate an effort and to work together. After all, mistakes *are* mistakes. My former attorneys had already consulted one of the most prestigious law firms in town. Battle lines had been drawn. My former attorneys were starting to circle the wagons.

"Okay, perhaps we should have filed the papers prior to April first. But if all the things we now know about Steve were known to us before, we would have had to make some kind of disclosure and he wouldn't have been able to put a deal together, anyway."

"Andy,* what are you talking about?" I shouted.

"You know full well what I'm talking about. You're not going to take me down the drain with you! I had no idea you were invading those limited partnership accounts prior to the closing."

"Why, you creep! Don't hand me that garbage! You *did* know about it. You knew I took it out of the partnership accounts. You needed me to pay your closing fees in advance because your lack of cash flow was going to put you under without my help! The advances were from the limited partnership accounts. And you mean to tell me you had no idea where the money kept coming from to extend the time on that aborted Cherokee deal? The checks I gave the seller for the extensions came from the partnership account and *you were the one who gave it to him.*"

"Lawson, you're crazy, and I don't know what you're talking about. Let's get one thing straight—your blood isn't on my hands. Whatever happens to you, you've brought it all on yourself without any help from me! Now get out of my office!"

"Yeah, I'll get out all right!" I fumed. "The stink around here is making me sick. You've always been a sanctimonious jerk, Andy, but I'll tell you one thing—if this is going to end up being a bloodbath, you're going to get as bloody as me."

My new attorneys spelled it out for me. I *did* have a problem, though at that time I could see only the tip of the iceberg. Since I did not fall under the private placement exemption a proper and timely filing would have afforded, I now came under the Federal Securities Act that required the sort of documentation and disclosure I was not required to give under a private placement.

"Listen . . . " I said. "It wasn't even my mistake. Surely they'll understand if we go to them and explain."

"True," my lawyers advised me, "but they'd demand you make a full offering circular of every investment you closed, and give the investors a copy."

"It will be expensive and a pain in the neck, but that's okay," I replied.

"Then you have to offer them a chance to rescind their investment, if they wish. Do you have money available to repay all who might like to get out?"

Of course I didn't. There was no way I could offer all those investors a chance to pull out of their investments. Of the monies collected, most went to the sellers at closing. Legal fees had also been paid. I shook my head.

"Stephen, you really have a problem," they offered soberly.

◆

I had two options, it appeared, and neither was pleasant. First, I could pretend I didn't have a problem at all; perhaps nothing would come of my former attorneys' oversight. That was potentially dangerous, however, in that any investor who wanted out and consulted an attorney might end up letting all the investors know they were entitled to a recision of their investment. A real estate recession had just begun in Atlanta, and investors might have leapt at such an opportunity.

My other option was to take the bold approach: simply go to the Securities and Exchange Commission and confess the error. I was encouraged to think that would impress the Commission, and that I would receive merely a slap on the wrist.

I decided to take the second approach, and my attorneys helped me prepare a disclosure document for the Federal Securities and Exchange Commission. I felt uncomfortable signing it, since it placed in writing the candid facts about the aborted closing and payback, along with facts concerning the Certificate of Deposit monies. I signed it and took it to the SEC, where I immediately knew I was in trouble. My heart sank as I realized that these officials did not deal in wrist slapping, but were serious as a heart attack about their intent to investigate my firm's irregular uses of clients' monies.

Despite my years of experience in explaining my way out of tight places, I had no desire to try to bluff or manipulate. The SEC investigated my firm for more than half a year with my full cooperation and disclosure of all requested facts. Meanwhile, my new attorneys advised me not to promote any other land ventures. My former attorneys were given good advice when told to get out of my boat. It was developing more leaks than I could begin to plug.

At last, on December 1, I received a phone call from the Commission. They'd received an order from Washington about me and my firm. The action would be limited to my signing a civil consent order saying I'd violate no security laws in the future.

My heart sang. Just a slap on the wrist, after all. Finally, the nightmare was over, and I could resume my business. I signed the papers, kept a copy for myself, and bade the SEC good-bye.

The next morning, as I read my newspaper, the bottom dropped out of my personal world. A news story and head-lines related that Stephen P. Lawson and Cambridge Capital Corporation had signed a consent order after admitting to fraud, and that a special fiscal agent of the court would run the affairs of the various partnerships.

As I read further, to my horror, I saw the story included details of my Certificates of Deposit scheme, and details of the aborted land closing. Nowhere did it mention that these people had been paid back at a handsome profit.

As quickly as my morning newspaper slid from my fingers, I realized I was out of business.

Though my business was effectively destroyed, it took months for it to die. For the remainder of that year and the next I worked with the special fiscal agent as investor meetings were held. Our investors had totally lost confidence and looked upon me as a "smoothie" who had taken their hard-earned money.

With each month that passed, my props began to go—the beautiful cars and elegant office, my public image, the bank accounts, our clients, my "friends," even those I had "loved" and lavishly entertained.

One investor approached me angrily, yelling that I could take his wife, but how dare I take his money! A close friend, more honest and direct, put it this way: "Steve, until this entire episode is behind you, I don't think we should see each other anymore."

I shouldn't be surprised at this sort of thing, I told myself. *Mother was right. A dollar really is your best friend, when all is said and done.*

In the end, all the investment groups went under, and I had been the single largest investor. I was broke and out of business. There was no reason to have an office when there were no investors, and there was no use having overhead when there was no way to pay the bills.

The first thing I did upon coming to this realization was to visit Don Patterson at the Edwards Baking company. Aside from wanting to interview for a position there, I was drawn to speak to Don for reasons I couldn't readily explain.

He had been an investor of mine and had referred others to me. All of them had lost money. Still, for some reason I approached Don with my problems, somehow knowing he'd be responsive. Also, I wanted him to know how sorry I was to have caused him so many problems. I was genuinely sorry for Don's losses.

Amazingly, Don hadn't seen the paper and knew nothing. He received the news without much display of emotion, considering he'd just learned that some $25,000 of his investments had gone down the tubes. I explained that I was broke and needed a job.

"How is Harvey? How's she talking all this?" Don asked. Then he reached into his desk drawer and wrote me a check for $5,000. "Steve, I hope this will help. You can pay me someday when you're able. Meantime, I'll set up some appointments for you here, though I can't guarantee you a position."

His attitude totally disarmed me. The hurts I'd sustained from other friends fled from my memory as I contemplated Don's calm and compassionate demeanor.

As I drove away, I tried to figure him out. During all our married life Harvey and I had known Don and Patti and, although we regularly swapped dinner invitations, you could hardly call us close friends. They made no bones about Christ being the center of their home. They acted, to my notion, like typical Bible Belt people, the sort who seem to have lived their lives without hatred, jealousy, or trauma, and have always had an excellent relationship with parents who adore them and would be offended if they didn't show up for Sunday brunch at the club. As I saw it, the God they thought was so marvelous must also be the same one who created acne, bad breath, athlete's foot, and caused your teeth to fall out of your head during old age.

At home, Harvey was equally impressed. That day she and I sat alone and talked a long time about the concerns that filled our life.

"We're about to go through some rough times," I told my wife. "I can remember when my folks went through some similar trials."

Through my mind's eye, I saw a montage of old horror scenes—my mother, contorted with fear, and my aging father, demoralized and hopeless, berating one another and at last turning on me. I panicked at the thought that my own adult life would mirror that of my parents. The unbearable things Mother had said to my father she had also said to me. He had died at last and gotten beyond the effect of those words—which at that moment were being revived. I tried to convey to Harvey the video replay that was going on inside me.

"Harvey, we must make a pledge to one another to be kind to each other at all times. Honey, I couldn't stand it if you were to become to me what Mother ended up being to my dad."

Harvey assured me. There were to be no recriminations. Whatever needed doing—even returning to work and leaving her eighteen-month-old baby—she did willingly and with a beautiful spirit.

———◆———

Lawsuits started pouring in. Each evening the doorbell rang, and the marshal served us with more. In all, I was to receive some $600,000 worth of lawsuits from former investors who sought rescission of their investments and return of all money invested, due to the missed filing date.

Missed filing date? I recognized that point as being merely a legal ruse. Each of these suits, I persuaded myself, indicated my clients' belief in me; they were lining up with me, against my attorneys.

In every case, as I answered the suits I brought my former attorneys in as third-party defendants. My posture was that if the investors held valid assumptions that I owed them money, it was due to my attorneys' malpractice. And attorneys have malpractice insurance. This "deep pocket" was what the investors were after.

I viewed these suits as a great opportunity for vindication. Should my attorneys be judged at fault by the legal process they served, I would consider that the ultimate vindication. I also sued my former attorneys for malpractice and punitive damages in excess of a million dollars. I believed, as did many others, that I *had* to win. It was an open-and-shut case.

For years we were to wage battle and for years I was to hate with all my heart. It would take nearly five years for me to understand that I must admit my own guilt and accept responsibility for my own actions.

Meanwhile, I clung to the belief that I could not possibly lose my lawsuits. Even if I did, however, my former attorneys would see their practice destroyed by rumors and idle talk—exactly as my business had been. They, too, depended upon referrals. Soon they'd be hurting financially. They would learn, as I had, that trying to stop a rumor was like trying to unring a bell.

I believed my hatred was justified. Not only had the attorneys erred initially in not filing the papers, but now they blamed me entirely. They claimed to know nothing about my past actions (such as co-mingled funds), though in fact they did. They stonewalled and lied, and I viewed their conduct as despicable.

While I devoted myself single-mindedly to my hatred, Harvey dealt with other, more immediate realities. I had no job and couldn't get one. Day by day, our prospects grew more nightmarish. As Harvey relates,

We had no business, no source of income, our investments were lost, the savings wiped out. We were jobless and without hope of any kind. I would wake in the night in a sweat, heart pounding, sure that I was having a nightmare, then remember that we were living a nightmare. It was obvious that I would have to go back to work, and immediately.

As I lost myself in hatred, Harvey was submerged in pain. Her notes reflect our general turmoil:

I hadn't lost only the material things. I was cut off from the very things that had given me my sense of identity and worthiness. Additionally, I had put all my energy, faith, and trust in Stephen. I had backed a winner and now he had lost—and lost big. It wasn't just the loss of money; we had lost our acceptability.

I perceived condemnation that was both real and imagined. I didn't want to go anywhere; I was sure even the grocery store manager had read the awful things about us in the newspapers. Certainly I couldn't go to any volunteer meetings. I even felt squeamish about walking the dog or seeing people in our condominium association.

Harvey found a job and returned to work. I learned that no one wants to hire a person with lawsuits pending and, after countless interviews, settled into the only job I could find—that of househusband in our own home.

It became my special time to be with Blake, a time few fathers ever experience. I believe the special bond between Blake and me was formed at that time.

Yes, there were advantages, but after two years in limbo I knew I needed to go back to work, and I needed it desperately.

So when Larry,* a former investor, phoned and wanted to get together, I found myself quite receptive.

Chapter 11

Undercover Work

There have been some forthright conversations in my life, but none quite so forthright as the one with Larry that afternoon. Larry was a successful physician in the greater Atlanta area. I could see that he intended to capitalize on my misfortune by helping me return to business, becoming my silent partner, and making a handsome profit for himself.

He had a simple plan. He knew a great number of physicians out of state, mostly in the Carolinas and in Florida. He'd send me to see them with rave reviews, declare he intended to become a principal investor in the land under discussion, and encourage their participation. Since they were out of state, they'd know nothing about me and my problems. We were confident that my salesmanship could handle potential objections of investing in Atlanta rather than in their own locales.

Never mind ethics. Strong hatred for my former attorneys and all others who were accessories to my downfall made me jump at Larry's suggestions. I was hungry and hurting. Larry's plan, motivated by greed and greased by deception, tied in with my own strong needs and motivations.

It had been more than two years since I'd made a living. My househusband duties had reached the point of diminishing returns and made it easy for me to justify violating my consent order. After all, hadn't my attorneys been the ones at fault? Despite that, it was *my* family who suffered. I'd show them; I'd make a successful comeback.

I had learned a great deal about the laws concerning securities. (Much more than I'd ever wanted to know, actually.) I realized I was violating my consent order in the most basic way by not providing potential investors with full disclosure. Full disclosure would dictate that I tell them all about the SEC action and the lawsuits pending, not to mention other negative details. The trouble was, such disclosure would mean I'd sell no units of ownership.

The answer? I had someone else serve as general partner, thus concealing from the securities authorities my involvements with these investments. The offering circulars sent to the state securities office in Atlanta were approved without delay. I honestly believed my actions would go undetected.

Armed with introductions that wouldn't fail, I drove to Florida to start a prolonged selling trip. I met many nice people who bought what they saw, and who invested willingly. I received their money with confidence that the investments were sound and that they'd eventually produce handsome profits. The land was purchased and I rationalized that the lack of disclosure to which these investors were entitled made no difference whatever, since they were going to make money.

I was getting back on my feet, making money again. I had leased a Mercedes-Benz so that the image of prosperity would be transmitted to any prospective investors. I had even begun to make an impression on myself. I believed I was planting seeds for an even more prosperous future than before.

From today's perspective, however, I see that God was allowing me those last yards of line, and I was playing myself out. I was like a fish who had been hooked, was fighting, unable to pull free, panicked and desperate and—using every last ounce of energy—finally must yield, and is pulled into the boat, exhausted.

Harvey was struggling in her own way:

It was good to see Stephen busy again. It was more than the fact he was putting together the finances of our life; he was the guy who I could truly depend on to overcome any obstacle—the sort of person described by the saying, "When life hands you a lemon, make lemonade." I was proud of him. Yet something deep inside told me that this was only temporary.

I couldn't help but remember the large beetle I had observed while sitting on a park bench one day. Somehow it had landed on its back and was using every bit of energy to right itself, knowing, I guess, that it would die in its present state. After ten minutes passed it turned over and started heading off the pavement to the grassy area. At that moment a child ran by and stepped on the beetle, killing it instantly. The child ran off, never knowing what had happened and the role she had played as terminator in that bug's life. I could only hope that somehow we wouldn't be like that bug—working so hard to survive only to have someone squash us.

I couldn't enjoy Stephen's comeback in the way I had shared in his original successes. What was the matter? Time would tell, I guessed.

I had left Palm Beach and was headed toward Lakeland, Florida. Previously I had met several doctors at a well-known clinic, and we were to meet again that afternoon. It was a beautiful day, and the road stretched in front of me like a ribbon for as far as I could see.

My thoughts, as usual, centered on my former attorneys, and I hoped it was true that "every turkey had its Thanksgiving." I contemplated the progress of the lawsuits and the upcoming deposition and then turned my full attention to hating them. The venom in my heart erupted through my body, and I was absolutely obsessed by the idea of coming up with a new way to do to them what they had done to me.

I turned on the radio and then put in a musical tape. I leaned back in the seat and tried to relax. My former attorneys might be worthy of all the emotional effort I was expending, but the effort was sapping and made me half crazy every time I directed thought to it.

Suddenly, the loneliness was upon me. I hadn't experienced it since having met Harvey some eleven years ago. As with the wind, I had no idea where it had come from, but it had returned—and the torment it produced was instantaneous.

These feelings of loneliness were incredible, and they came at the craziest times. I could have understood having those kinds of emotions when I was alone or during moments of sadness or disappointment. But it was never depression; it was a feeling of being totally alone in life without anyone caring about me or loving me. And with it came the desperate, oppressive feeling that there was absolutely no hope of change or recovery.

It always came without warning. One minute I was fine, the next consumed by the sense of total alienation and would remain so for the next few days. I could be the life of the party somewhere (as I often was), and on the spot become the most desolate person in the room. My outward persona never changed, since I was a great actor and could carry on for the entire evening as though nothing were wrong. But something *was* wrong—everything was wrong.

Had I possessed the keys to the kingdom of Heaven it-self, I would have given them up in a New York minute in order to relieve that loneliness permanently.

In earlier years I had considered that part of it had to do with being single—having no roots or place to really belong. But this was no longer the case; I had a wife who was enviously beautiful, charming, and loving. Why this onslaught of feelings now?

I no longer heard the tape player, and I could hardly drive the car. Instead of driving it with confidence, I was merely aiming it in an attempt to keep it on the road. There were no other cars within sight, and the road was as straight as an arrow. Nevertheless, all coordination had deserted me and fear for my life encompassed me. Despite the emotional storm raging within, I continued to drive. Every hurt, bad experience, and pathos I had known filled these moments of loneliness.

At that point God was starting to take the initiative in bringing me to himself. For some reason, at that moment I looked up over the horizon into the clouds and said, "Jesus, please help me. I can do anything on my own, but I can't handle these feelings of loneliness, and I ask you to take them from me." Without realizing it, I had admitted that Jesus was Lord and that he was fully capable of taking my pain from me if I asked. At that time, spiritual discernment was beyond me. All I knew was that within an instant the loneliness had departed. Not only had it departed, but I felt better than I had in years. I had been road weary, having been away from home for about two weeks. Now it was as if I had just had a marvelous night's sleep and awoke to a hot shower. I felt fresh—invigorated. When a person has been met at the very point of his need, it tends to grab his attention. The experience I have just related might not seem like a miracle to some, but it certainly qualified as one in my view.

My meetings in Lakeland concluded successfully, I drove on to Gainesville and arrived in the early evening. I hadn't told anyone about my experience yet, so I called Harvey.

"You won't believe what happened to me on the road today . . ." I began. The event unfolded and, strangely, there wasn't much of a response on the other end of the phone.

"Honey, how interesting. Are you feeling okay now?" She said, changing the subject.

"Yeah, I feel fine."

I got off the phone with Harvey and sat on the edge of the bed. It hadn't been a very satisfying conversation. Who could I share it with who might see the significance in what happened like I did—whatever it was?

Of course. The Pattersons. I smiled and dialed the number. Patti's cheerful voice flooded my ear.

"Hi, Patti. It's Steve Lawson."

"Hi, Steve! How are you?" Patti always has had a knack for making a person feel that she has been sitting by the phone waiting for his call.

I explained where I was, that I was on business, but something had happened I had to tell them about. "I think I had a religious experience. It was the darnedest thing that ever happened in my entire life."

She was definitely interested. I related what had happened, giving her some background on my bouts of severe loneliness. The only thing I didn't admit was how unusual it was for me to have uttered Jesus' name. The Pattersons didn't know I was Jewish any more than anyone in my Southern circle of acquaintances.

"Oh Steve, that's *wonderful!*"

"What do you make of it?" I asked.

"I don't know, other than to say that I think the Lord is trying to tell you he loves you."

This was a typical Patti Patterson response. All the times before her religious jargon had turned me off completely. But it didn't seem to bother me so much this time. Then she asked if we could pray. I said I didn't mind, more to be polite than anything else. And so she prayed—a prayer I only half listened to. Hidden in this prayer it seemed that she was delicately preaching a message to me. Finally, she finished, and we hung up. *She's a religious flake,* I thought. *She said that Don would still be at the office. He'll have some straight talk for me.* I phoned him, and we talked for about fifteen minutes. It was obvious that somehow Patti had tipped him off to our conversation, because he didn't seem at all surprised, and his answers were much the same as hers. But I knew that they couldn't have talked, because I had dialed him directly after speaking with her and had reached him without delay.

After our conversation, I came across a *Good News for Modern Man* Bible sitting on the table next to the phone. On the cover there was an explanation that the Bible was a gift from the people at Days Inn and an invitation for me to take it with me when I left.

I praise God today not only for the ministry of that company that used to place a Bible in each room, but also that it was an easy-to-understand version. I picked up the Bible and quickly looked through it. It was a New Testament. *This is the one with Jesus all through it, the testament that Jews don't acknowledge. Hmmm.* I sat down in a chair and started to read at the beginning—Matthew.

"This is the genealogy of Jesus Christ . . ."

"Boy, it doesn't take them long to get into it, does it!" I said laughingly. I closed the book, leaving my fingers by the page I had started.

"Dear God," I prayed as best I knew how, "if you are really who you say you are and Jesus is really who he said he was, and if this book is really your inspired Word, well . . . then I'm going to commit myself to reading it. But the rest is up to you. Amen." After all, it was honest to let him know where I stood.

I leaned back, got comfortable, and started reading the book. I knew nothing at all about Jesus and had never been in church to hear the gospel, much less read any Scripture. I didn't even realize what a Gospel was, much less that there were four or what they were about, or who they were written to or by.

After a while I realized that for a person who never read much, I had been totally engrossed in reading the Bible for three hours. I was starving. I got in the car and headed for a nearby restaurant. I would read, question, and consider Jesus for the next two and a half years before I asked him into my heart. But the journey that would change my life had begun—and somehow I knew I was much like the person Jesus had met on the path who had been blind from birth. Jesus had touched him, and he was never the same. When questioned the man said that a man had done it. Later he was to say that Jesus was a prophet. Later still he would call him Lord. Yes, something had happened on that road, like it or not. But maybe I was making too much of it. At that point all I knew was that I was going to continue to read that Bible as soon as I returned from dinner.

On Friday afternoon, following my road experience, I hurried toward Atlanta and the people I loved most—Harvey and Blake. All that travel was getting old. When I got honest with myself, I had to admit that doing business on the sly held little satisfaction. Success was hollow. It was great to pay the bills again, true, but apart from that the work generated very little personal satisfaction. I couldn't help but remember the old days of additional cash back in New York.

I'd make some money with the bookmaker, but couldn't let any of it show because of my folks. Now I had to adopt a low profile because of the SEC and unresolved lawsuits from former investors. History had repeated itself.

That evening, Tim & Alice Jones* arrived for dinner. They are such comfortable people, and we always enjoyed being in their company. I thought that Harvey's choice of dinner and friends, in honor of my first night back, was wonderful.

"Say Tim, did Harvey mention what happened to me on the road this week?" I asked.

"No, what do you mean?"

"I was driving between Palm Beach and Lakeland," the story began. Some twenty minutes later, I'd recounted it all. Tim had interrupted several times to exclaim, "You don't say!" and Alice had remarked, "Oh, my word." All was silent at the other end of the table, however.

Harvey had heard the story before, of course. She had been silent when I told it by telephone, but now I was with her and could read her face and mood. It was clear that she wanted to change the subject, and she managed to do so in short order.

The following week I shared my Florida experience with several other couples, and each time Harvey added nothing but a quiet display of annoyance. After I'd related the story for perhaps the fourth time, she could stand it no longer.

"Listen, Stephen," she warned me one evening as we prepared for bed, "I've had it with this Jesus stuff."

"What are you talking about?" I queried.

"You know, that road story you keep telling. I've absolutely had it and I want to tell you, Mister, that if you don't stop this Jesus business, I'm going to wring your neck."

She wasn't kidding. You could tell by the way she said it that the conversation was closed. There was nothing left to discuss, and if I were smart I'd agree with her and never tell that story again. Any time Harvey injects the word "Mister" into a sentence, you know you're skating on very thin ice. But I wasn't that smart.

"Can I please ask what in the world you're talking about?" I asked.

"Look, I think it's absurd that a Jewish man is sitting at a dinner table, night after night, talking about Jesus Christ and what happened to him on the road. Aside from that, you and I have always been best friends, and I'm not going to risk your becoming a religious fanatic like the Pattersons."

"Harvey, I think you've lost your mind! I know I'm Jewish, and if you think I'm going to become a Jesus freak, then you're crazier than I ever thought you could get."

"Then why do you bring it up so often, and why are you starting to read the Bible?"

"First of all, Honey, I've never read it before," I said. "All of our Atlanta friends are Gentiles, and I'm curious to know their beliefs. I'd like to have some background so I don't sound as stupid in conversation as they do sometimes when they refer to Jews."

"Are you sure that's it?"

"Of course. I can't see why you'd even consider me a prospect for this stuff," I reassured her, believing every word I said. "It isn't compatible for me as a Jew, and I wouldn't desecrate Dad's memory for anything. You know that. Also, I wouldn't say the secret way I'm going about making a living is something I care to sit down and discuss with God!"

We both laughed, and the tension was broken.

Harvey, however, continued to turn to me from time to time, saying in her way that she had reached the end of her inner resources. She described it this way:

I threw myself into my job and let it overcome and possess me. While Stephen was obsessed with legalities, hatred for his former attorneys, and the need for justification at any cost, I became obsessive/compulsive about my work.

Desperately lonely in that job, alienated and cast aside from old friends and without the time, desire, or opportunity to develop new ones, I shared all my needs and concerns with Stephen. I told him how lonely and lost I was. I told him I felt like a spent piece of elastic; I couldn't spring back anymore.

Stephen tried to help. It isn't that he wouldn't; he couldn't. I couldn't listen to the constant talk regarding the legalities, and Stephen couldn't talk about anything else. We went through the motions of sharing and talking as we always had done, but neither of us could hear the other's cry for help.

We were hopelessly lost, trying to control our own lives, which were destined for disaster, using all the old techniques we had used successfully in the past but that no longer worked.

My phone calls to Patti and Don had jolted them both into action on my behalf. Harvey and I became permanent fixtures on the prayer list posted on Patti's refrigerator door. Books began appearing in our mailbox, such as *Evidence That Demands a Verdict*, though we never saw them placed there. Frankly, I found the books quite interesting, and began to phone Don fairly often to ask questions about this point or that.

The books, phone calls, questions, and study continued on an irregular basis for two and a half years. Once Don had me meet him at his office so I could meet his prayer partner, who Don claimed could answer some of my tougher questions.

I read those books faithfully, almost every night. Occasionally I missed one evening's reading because I couldn't find the books—and knew Harvey had hidden them again. Or if she hadn't hidden them, they certainly weren't in the same place twice.

◆

The deposition with my former attorneys took place in the offices of one of Atlanta's leading law firms. It looked like a bar convention. Every lawyer representing clients in various suits against me had arrived, wanting to question my former attorneys.

Not only did most people perceive those hated attorneys of mine to be at fault, but in my third partying all the suits to them, it represented the deep pocket everyone hoped to find. They carried malpractice insurance, after all. At last they were on display, and my vengeful moment of truth had arrived.

As we gathered, I found a quiet corner to myself. It was time for my third prayer. My first had occurred on the road to Lakeland, the second prior to my reading the Bible in the motel room in Gainesville.

I lowered my head and leveled with God. "You know how much I hate these attorneys. Without your help, I won't be able to handle it. Unless you calm me I'm afraid I'll jump over the conference table and strangle the no-good

——. If what happened in Florida was really you, I need your help. I pray this *in the name of Jesus*. Amen."

Later at home I knew that—like it or not—Harvey had to hear what happened. I told her what I'd done, how I'd prayed in the name of Jesus, and what had transpired.

"I was cool as a cucumber," I testified in disbelief. "They sat there and lied about one thing after another. Believe it or not, I never got upset, and I even felt compassion. I'm sorry for their families. I don't want them to suffer the way you and Blake have suffered—I mean, the wives and the kids, they haven't done anything to us. It was a miracle. A first-class miracle. I don't see how I could be in the same room with them . . . listening to the false statements . . . suddenly it didn't matter anymore. That was the first miracle. The second happened while they questioned one of those guys. There he was, in the hot seat where I wanted him, trying to answer questions . . . and he started to cough and choke. Harvey, I got up from that table and brought him a Coke. Can you imagine! I don't know whose compassion that was, but it sure wasn't mine. I don't have one ounce of compassion for those creeps."

Harvey studied me closely, trying to understand, but I couldn't explain what had happened to me. I only knew the stench of the hatred I'd nurtured every day for the past five years, that hatred that motivated almost every thought and action of my life, simply evaporated the moment I called upon the name of Jesus.

I didn't understand it at all. I was totally unaware that God was drawing me to himself, step by step.

Chapter 12

The Breaking of a Man

At last, things were looking up. My business increased, and I justified taking prime office space within the Omni International Complex in downtown Atlanta. I still gambled, but otherwise my problems seemed far less formidable.

Anyone would have enjoyed having office space at the Omni, but I had a singular advantage there—that of close proximity to the attorneys I loved to hate. Sometimes I'd be granted a chance run-in with one or the other and could toss off hateful one-liners: "You boys still in business?" "Do you still live in Atlanta?" Or, "Hello, George,* how's tricks?" I found that petty spite could be gratifying. I had read in the paper the previous week that George was one of six people being considered to fill the vacant position of Judge of the Northern District of Georgia. What pleasure I took in writing each member of the selection panel that George should not be considered a candidate while a suit filed over two years ago claiming legal malpractice was still not settled. I expressed my shock and dismay at George's *lack of full disclosure* to them and that George should now consider withdrawing his name. I knew it would eat George's heart out, (and Andy's, too, since they were partners) that I would be the one to lecture on lack of full disclosure. I loved it!

A few months later when someone else had been named to the post and I knew George had read the copy of the letter to the selection committee, which I had mailed him of course, I relished our chance meetings. "George, I'm so sorry you didn't get that Judgeship. Do you think there was a fly in the ointment, somewhere?"

Then, on the morning of May 14, 1978, a telephone call came I shall never forget. I recognized the voice—Gary Eubanks, attorney for numerous individuals who had filed suits against me and my former attorneys. Despite our adversarial positions, I liked and respected Gary. He represented his clients very well.

His voice sounded serious, even urgent. "Steve, I hate to call you so early in the morning with bad news, but I'm sure it's information you need."

I was instantly alert. Gary was not prone to overstatement.

"I learned last night that an assistant U.S. attorney is seeking information about you."

"What does that mean?"

"Well, she wouldn't be eliciting information about you unless she planned to take it to the Grand Jury for the purpose of indicting you."

All the blood seemed to drain from my head. Nausea swept over me, and my body tingled. When I thanked Gary and hung up the phone, I tried to calm myself . . . analyze the situation . . . get a handle on the fear that had taken hold of me.

What did those people want? There's no way they could know about my recent activities. Perhaps they had stumbled onto it by some fluke, yet I was confident I had covered my tracks extremely well.

They'd talked to an old investor, so they must have spoken about matters I'd called to the SEC's attention nearly five years before. Five years! That was it! The five-year statute of limitations on securities violations was nearly up; they must have pulled my file for one last look.

They could have brought criminal proceedings against me five years ago, had they desired. Why now? What was going to happen to me?

I immediately dialed the phone number of the U.S. Attorney's office.

"My name is Stephen Lawson, and I just received information that someone in your office is inquiring about me. I'd like to speak to that person, please."

After a few moments, we were connected. "Mr. Lawson, would you like to make a statement of any kind?"

"No, except that I have nothing to hide and will cooperate with you in every way. Whatever problems I had are past. You know I voluntarily went to the SEC about five years ago."

"Do you have an attorney, Mr. Lawson?"

"I know one I could phone, but I'm not represented at the moment."

"Mr. Lawson, I'd suggest you get one. Good day."

The click of the phone signaled the beginning of worse things to come. That afternoon my attorney called back to say he'd had a lengthy chat at the U.S. Attorney's office, and indeed I had problems. Not current problems, as I'd already figured out, but those old matters I'd disclosed years ago. Now they were intent on seeking an indictment.

At his office, my attorney spelled out the situation in more grim detail. "I'm most concerned because they have your confession on that disclosure document you signed with the SEC five years ago," he said. "It leaves us no defense. Aside from that, your fight now is with the Feds. Even if you won, the State securities people could come after you, state by state, because you had investors in so many states. It would be lengthy and costly—a blood bath, even if you won." He went on to say that our best strategy was for me to plead guilty and see if we could work out a deal.

Back at my office, I looked and felt like a walking corpse. I knew I was a finished man. My life was over. Every day for the past five years I'd fought battles real and imagined. But I couldn't fight this.

I dreaded breaking this news to Harvey. "Honey," I told her, sounding as though I was speaking from a bad dream, "it looks as though the SEC isn't through with me."

As I talked through the whole mess with her at home that day, the tears began to flow. For the next several days I couldn't look at Harvey without bursting into tears. I felt unbearable shame about the grief I'd caused my family. I had become everything my mother had said I would.

She said I would fail, and I *had* failed. I had failed myself and my family far beyond what my mother likely had pictured. As she had always predicted, if I were to approach any kind of success at all, surely I'd push the destruct button and somehow manage to fail. She said I'd end up like Dad. She was right.

In the following days I cried more tears than I thought any person could possess. Harvey and I stopped trying to have conversations because I would break down hopelessly. And she wasn't in much better shape. On May 17 and 18, I had previously planned investor get-togethers in Lexington, Kentucky. Harvey suggested that I keep that appointment, since perhaps each of us needed to be alone for a while. "We aren't doing much talking anyhow," she pointed out.

I agreed, for other reasons. Lexington was as good a place as any to kill myself.

That thought had faintly flickered through my mind at first, but soon I began to believe it presented the best way out—not just for me, but for Harvey and Blake. I realized that kind of legacy was no way for a man to honor his young son, but having your father in jail is no great legacy, either.

If I went to jail, Harvey would surely divorce me and, in time, marry someone else. That would destroy me. At least with this approach Harvey would acquire considerable life insurance proceeds so she could start her life anew. The two-year incontestability period for suicide (included in all life-insurance policies, meaning that no benefits will be paid in the event of suicide until two years after the policy has been issued) had long passed.

Yes, to kill myself would represent for each of us the least of all the evils. As long as Harvey would remarry anyway, at least she could have enough money to prevent her from marrying someone else just for the sake of his providing for them.

Blake wouldn't remember me when he grew up. I could imagine him telling people close to him, "I don't remember my real father at all. He committed suicide when I was four. Mom remarried, and as far as I'm concerned, *he's* always been a dad to me."

Darkness engulfed me. Satan, disguising my pride, ego, and selfishness as honor, integrity, and responsibility, lured me closer and closer to the edge of self-destruction.

These morbid thoughts were heightened by my absolute refusal to endure public scorn a second time, or to go to prison. No, I couldn't do it. Dead men are never indicted.

My decision was the only possible decision, and I'd enact it quickly.

In Lexington, the night before my scheduled meetings, I perfected my plans. One of my investors owned a sporting goods store, and I'd buy a gun there first thing in the morning. Sleep didn't come. I was imprisoned in my hotel room, waiting through one of those nights that took forever to turn into dawn. I tossed, turned, and sobbed. I had to do something. If I'd had a gun, it would have been the "right time."

I considered phoning Harvey, but I had nothing to say, and it was silly to wake her, in the event she was able to sleep. The note I'd leave would say it all, anyhow. Oh, how I loved her. Would she ever forgive me? Could she go through the rest of her life without hating me? Dear God, what had I done to her?

The clock read 3:00 A.M. It would be six or seven hours before I could buy the gun. Things I'd read and thought about . . . books Don Patterson had left in my mailbox . . . arguments about Jesus and the Bible . . . prayers . . . flooded into my consciousness. Turning over a new leaf wasn't what was needed—but a *new life*. Not merely repentance but regeneration. I dropped to my knees before the sofa and rested my elbows on the seat, with my head buried in my hands. I began to speak through my sobs.

"Dear God, I can't do it anymore. I have no fight left, and I'm going to kill myself. . . . I know that Jesus was your Son, I've read enough to believe that. You know how much I loved Dad, how I don't want to desecrate his memory . . . but I don't think this does. If anything would, it's the shame I've brought to his name through all these things I've done.

"Lord, I've had a life of successes and failures like anyone else. But now I'm at the end of my rope. Please hear my prayer, come into my heart, and make me a new person. I have nothing to give you, but please take me anyway. I want to be a Christian. Thank you, Father. It's *in the name of Jesus* that I pray."

I didn't feel better immediately. The hotel room still felt like a prison, containing one desperate, exhausted inmate. Only later would I realize that the continual sobbing had dwindled to intermittent tears. Also, I'd forgotten all about the sporting goods store. I returned home to Harvey.

◆

At home, my general mood was one of frustration and anger. For a long time I'd admired the Pattersons, their character and their lifestyle, yet I'd invited Jesus into my life and nothing had happened. I didn't feel one bit different.

I asked Harvey to phone the Pattersons and tell them we had to see them *tonight*. I told Harvey that I had prayed to become a Christian. That blockbuster didn't produce the hostile response I'd expected. Perhaps she hurt too much to care anymore, or maybe she was just walking through the final stages of our marriage and life together.

She didn't have the old fight, either. She appeared to be calm, but I guessed it was controlled hysteria. I couldn't blame her. When Patti and Don greeted us at the door they could tell that we weren't there for small talk. We were quickly ushered to a table beside their swimming pool, and Patti brought glasses of lemonade from the pool house. We talked, but Harvey remained quiet.

I could see that she was as numb as I was, and that she was present only because I had insisted. Out of love for me she was willing to try anything. At that point I was sure our marriage would not survive all this, and that Harvey was doing the things that would allow her to look back some-day and say she'd done everything she could.

The Pattersons listened intently as I told all about my life and the events of the past several days. I wept the entire time. At last I concluded my tirade, saying, "I asked Jesus to come into my life, and I don't feel any different. What did I do wrong? Is there a spiritual protocol I don't know about?"

For the first time I was asking Don questions he couldn't answer, and that upset me.

"I know God chooses us and not the other way around," I continued. "Could it be that I want him, but he doesn't want me?"

I had experienced the rejection of friends and, before that, the condemnation of my own mother. Apparently I could surmount those things, but a knowledge, borne on a tide of deep grief, made me think that God's rejection would be the final, unbearable indictment.

Don and Patti answered unhesitatingly that that could not be a possibility. Then Patti turned to Harvey. "Harvey, what do you think about what Steve has done? What's *your* reaction?"

It was the first time Harvey had been invited to speak. She'd sat there all this time, watching the way one might if caught at a location where two cars sped full throttle towards one another.

"Fine, I guess," she said. "I asked Jesus into my life, too, the other night."

I stared at her in disbelief. *Harvey?* I might have been an unlikely candidate for knowing the Lord, but Harvey was even more so.

Patti and Don brightened up at that. "Tell us about it!" Patti said.

"My feelings have been much the same as Stephen's. Last night while he was in Lexington, I couldn't sleep. At three in the morning I was wide awake and lying there scared, contemplating the future. I was soaked with perspiration, so I got up to take a shower. I bowed my head so the water could hit the back of my neck, and suddenly found myself on my knees. That's when I asked Jesus to come into my life . . . Apparently Stephen and I did it within fifteen minutes of each other."

"And how do *you* feel, Harvey?" asked Patti.

"Pretty much the same as he does. Nothing much."

Soon we left, taking our frustrations with us. As we pulled out of the Pattersons' driveway, I told Harvey angrily, "Whatever it was I expected to find by coming here tonight, I sure didn't get it. This whole thing must be a bunch of garbage. There may be a God and Jesus may be his Son, but they're surely not interested in me."

The next morning Harvey and I arose at our usual time. Something felt different. Something *was* different. Though we each realized it, we tried to analyze the feeling before being bold enough to share it with the other.

At last, Harvey spoke. "Honey, we weathered the other deal, and we'll weather this one, too. Let's face it together."

Those were the first positive words either of us had uttered in days. As we continued to speak, we realized what had happened—God had infused us with the Holy Spirit. Our sadness had begun to turn into joy. The bitterness turned into love, and the trauma to peace. Defeat became hope. We had been given his free gift of faith, filled to the brim and overflowing. I had begun to forgive, and I felt completely forgiven by God and by Harvey.

Now there was reason not only to live, but to rejoice. For the next three months Harvey and I stayed on a "high" from which it seemed we'd never descend. One day, as we left a department store, Harvey said she'd just met an old friend, who told her she looked wonderful.

"You know, I should have said, 'Why shouldn't I look good? My husband is going to the slammer, and we're broke,' " Harvey joked, her blue eyes dancing. Then she was suddenly wistful. "Do you think we'll go through life like this . . . so happy?"

I knew exactly what she meant. "Why didn't we accept Jesus years ago?" The truth was clear: *I had been in prison all my life, and now I was free.*

I read the Bible voraciously. Each page seemed to have been written especially to me. My prayer life was beyond any description I could give it. I didn't pray for needs as much as having the desire and joy of being in conversation with God.

Chapter 13

Grace Period

The Sunday following our conversation with the Pattersons, the leader of the adult Sunday school class at the Episcopal Cathedral of St. Philip asked if anyone had something to share. Like a shot, I stood and told everyone what had happened to Harvey and me. This was our first time in years to attend church other than for a holiday or a baptism. We were visitors in this class. But the newfound life and joy overcame any shyness I might have had otherwise.

I admitted I was Jewish and confessed that I'd hidden that fact in the past, but told everyone I was proud to be a *completed* Jew. Now I understood that Jews had not only been given a birthright but also the power to choose. There was a difference between Jews as they had evolved in their religious history and how the Lord had intended them to be. I told them that I chose to be chosen—chosen to be an heir with Christ. It was the first of many such testimonies I'd give in the months to come.

Harvey and I received a tremendous hunger for the Word of God. We were enthusiastic about opportunities for Bible study, prayer groups, teaching ministries, and occasions to witness. It was a great experience to share as a couple our first adventures with God.

Meanwhile, my attorney and I continued to grapple with my problems with the U.S. Attorney's office. I tried to find ways to earn money to provide for Harvey and Blake, should I go to prison, but nothing turned up. At the same time, I was compiling a long list of those persons I knew I had wronged and to whom I must go to ask their forgiveness. Those visits were never easy, yet each time I did what Jesus commanded, I was blessed far more than I could have expected.

Don Patterson suggested that I write to my former attorneys and ask for their forgiveness. I resisted; those years of intense, unrelenting, murderous hatred were hard to relinquish. But I knew Don was right. How could I *not* forgive, when I had been forgiven so much? But it was more than that. Even though these two men weren't Christians, the Lord had used them in such a powerful way to bring me to the end of myself. Was there any way to tell them that *overnight* my feelings of hatred had turned to love, and that they were constantly in my prayers? I agreed to compose the letter and read it to Don before mailing it.

In truth, I could apologize to those attorneys and former enemies for many of my actions, but there were things, in good conscience, for which I could *not* apologize. Wrestle though I might, I knew the key was *forgiveness*. The moment I dropped the letters in the mailbox a tremendous weight lifted off my heart. And I wept there—right on the street corner.

Later, George's and Andy's comments were passed back to me regarding my letters to them: "Tom* is a great criminal attorney and knows what he's doing. Lawson is capable of anything at this point, but this religious cop-out is a defense I wouldn't have figured him for." They remained convinced that I fully deserved to go to prison.

My new attorney and old friend was frank with me. "Steve, I shouldn't be saying this and don't intend to elaborate, but you wouldn't be going through all this if you hadn't gone for those two guys' jugular veins. For a number of years you have acted on the most base sort of emotions; they haven't. They understand the law and how the system works. You thought you were sticking it to them when all the time they were beating you to death."

As these various events transpired, Harvey and I began to know and love one another in a whole new dimension, that of the Spirit of God. The love we'd always had for one another paled in comparison to this new love we shared together in Christ. There came a fresh intimacy, great and precious, a bond that only Christian husbands and wives can understand.

We marveled at being captured by Christ—separately, but on the same day, even the same hour! As Harvey described it:

I didn't come to the Lord because of Stephen's problems. I had my own conflicts, turmoil, and shortcomings. I had become as desperate as he. He had been my best friend. We were a fortress unto ourselves. When we lost our money, for the most part we lost our friends. We vowed to be kind to one another in spite of everything. My confidante was and is Stephen.

Blake, the joy of our lives, was two weeks old when Stephen's house of cards collapsed. Blake was fourteen months old when I had to return to work, and I have always regretted that.

As time went on, Stephen and I talked about nothing but litigation—what might happen, our chances to be restored. The hatred boiling in Stephen affected me deeply. His poison fed me, too. I had begun to develop a hard edge. I saw Blake's babyhood slipping away, my husband involved in one horrible problem after another, and loneliness almost destroyed me.

I began to jog each night, hoping to dissolve some of my tension and desperate unhappiness. As I ran, I tried to clear my head. I'd talk to God, a God I doubted was there. I told him how much Stephen's indictment scared me, that I needed help. How I wished there was someone with whom I could converse about ordinary things.

Oh, I was so scared and vulnerable. Scared of losing Stephen as well as myself. I didn't think God was listening. I had become cynical. One night I told him, "If you are God, prove that I can run a mile without stopping." I felt an invisible hand in the middle of my back, pushing. I ran that mile, and kept on going.

That's the way it was, until that night in the shower. The morning after our visit with the Pattersons, we both entered into perfect peace.

Three weeks after I became a Christian, I attended a prayer group where a person mentioned something called the "baptism in the Holy Spirit."

"If there is something *more*," I blurted, "I want it!" The next day several Christian brothers met with me and prayed me through deliverance, inner healing, and the empowering from God's Spirit. I was freed that day from a lot of the sludge of my past life.

Two weeks later, Harvey was freed in the same way. We didn't see then the importance of God's timing. He was preparing us, strengthening us, and setting our feet on a firm place. Soon would come trials that the old Steve and Harvey could not have endured.

On May 27, 1978, Harvey and I were given the sacrament of water baptism by an ordained minister in the Pattersons' swimming pool, and they presented me with a new Bible— one that is held together today by rubber bands because it's had so much use.

Those first seven months following my conversion, I lived in a kind of euphoria. Both Harvey and I saw the world through fresh eyes. We were filled with joy and gratitude. At last I had accepted myself—my failures, problems, and sins—because I had accepted Christ to be the guide of my life. And I was even more interested in learning about the God who had freed me, since he was also the God of my Jewish heritage.

For the first time, my life had a transparency—no more clouded words, disguises, ambiguous and deceptive meanings. Since I wasn't afraid of who I was, I could *be* myself.

More and more, I was given opportunities to give my Christian testimony. At those times, Satan would attack. I'd feel such pain in my knees and ankles that on many occasions I'd have to drag myself to the car. By the time I spoke, however, the pain would be gone. There are two things the evil one detests: first, for a person to become a Christian; and second, for that person to become an *effective* Christian.

One evening Harvey and I had decided to see a movie— not a frequent event for us. We were primed for a light, fun-filled evening. Armed with popcorn and Cokes, we settled back to enjoy a very funny film. And the movie was living up to our expectations, except that after the first half hour, I didn't see it.

Suddenly, I was alone with Satan. It was like being in an isolation booth. I heard no sounds, and though I watched the screen, I didn't comprehend what I saw. All I knew was that *I had to kill myself.*

There was no logical thought process to this, as there had been when I was back in Lexington, months ago. I simply felt an overpowering compunction to kill myself *right now.*

I couldn't utter a sound. My entire attention focused on *getting it done.* How? Where? Had there been a gun in my car, I'm sure I would have left the theater right then and killed myself in the parking lot. Prayer was beyond my grasp.

Somehow, I started breathing the name of Jesus. *Jesus, Jesus, Jesus,* over and over again. The war seemed to go on forever. The movie ended, I saw the lights come on, and

Harvey and I moved from the theater amidst a stream of other people. Outside, in hurried expressions of distress, I turned to her and blurted out what was happening to me.

We sat in the car and prayed, talked, then prayed some more. We left the parking lot, stopped at a gas station for a fill-up, and ended up in a restaurant, where we talked for hours.

From the time we entered the restaurant, the ominous feelings were gone; in fact, I'd never felt better. But that experience drove home a point for me, and gave some insight to a question that I often hear: "Can a person who is a Christian commit suicide?" The devil is real and will pound at our weaknesses. That night could have turned out differently. It strengthens me to know that Jesus came to destroy the works of the devil (1 John 3:8).

As the storm clouds of my life moved in rapidly during May, 1978, I realized that my conversion to Christ was for me and me alone. The condemnation from other Jews was more than I can easily express. Moreover, even Christians had suspicions about the veracity of someone who might be grasping at straws, "in the name of the Lord," because he appeared to be on his way to jail. For the first time, I consciously decided to place my eyes on God, and on how *God* saw me, rather than worry about what people might think. And for the first time, appearance and impressions cut no ice whatever. It was just the new me out there, for people to see and judge as they would. I was out of the impressions business—no more slick talk and put-on personality.

Later I would discover that my commitment made me a partner with Jesus, and I would discover union with him. I would find him to be all I needed and desired. He would prove himself faithful, sufficient, forgiving, merciful, and just. I knew, without a doubt, that my salvation was proof that the gospel is valid in modern-day life.

And later I would more fully understand that I had been forgiven completely and that I was truly reconciled to my heavenly Father. He was equipping me, through Jesus, to be the man who, on my own, I had no power, ability, or authority to be.

It didn't happen at once—that understanding. It took time to firmly establish the facts in a mind and heart that had been conditioned to believe and see in other ways. Jesus really did take my place when he died on Calvary. Satan had been beaten. After a time, even that enemy could not convince me that my sins still stood in the way; I was certain, heart and soul, that all my wrongs had been canceled by God.

I had been through a breaking period, when everything had fallen apart. I had been hopeless; now I experienced the power of God's grace, grounded in the knowledge provided in the previous two and a half years of reading and study. I had called out to the Lord, and he heard—and delivered me from my fears.

Chapter 14

Without One Plea

Tim and Alice invited us for lunch at the Commerce Club. They were to stand with Harvey and me at the time of my sentencing, and Tim wanted to say a few words on my behalf to the judge.

These were close, comfortable friends with whom we had always shared New Year's Eve. Both Harvey and Alice are exceptional cooks, and we'd feasted on many gourmet dinners at our house or theirs. Once we had vacationed together in Bermuda.

Tim and Alice stuck with us when my business went under in 1974, when I couldn't pay the rent, and when there were no funds for insurance payments. They stood by when I entered my consent order with the Securities and Exchange Commission, and when I learned I would be indicted. Still they were our friends, sharing a special lunch and a monumental concern over one more tough event—my sentencing.

After I became a Christian, I was eager to bring all the dark deeds to light. At one point, my attorney had said that I actually might win this case in court. He would have to depend on the U.S. Attorney's overtrying her case, which he felt she was likely to do.

The problem with that, I explained, was that I was guilty as charged. I wanted to embark on my new life in Christ with old things truly past. That meant I must even admit to things the court knew nothing about and would depend on God to watch over me as I revealed the truth.

For years I had fought one battle after another—with the SEC, my former attorneys, old investors—and I had no desire to fight another. My attorney promised to do the very best he could and advised me not to worry about the expense. He knew I had no money; he agreed to receive payment at some future time.

I wish I could relate that it was easy to plead guilty, but it was not. The government originally was willing to accept my pleading guilty to two counts. Now, with new information, the government insisted on raising the ante. I would plead guilty to three counts. It took nearly ten months to agree on the litany of those crimes that, in good conscience, I could plead. Discussion after discussion took place in the U.S. Attorney's offices. I gave the Assistant U.S. Attorney private seminars on real estate so she could have the general background necessary to understand how my crimes were committed, of what I was clearly guilty, and of what I was clearly innocent. At last we agreed, and I signed the plea admitting my guilt.

Thus I had drawn a line that separated the new Stephen Lawson from the old. The old Stephen had been another person. Many months later, in a news magazine, I came across a statement from former president Richard Nixon that delineates so well my former thinking and actions:

> What starts the process, really, are laughs and slights and snubs when you are a kid . . . If your anger is deep enough and strong enough, you learn that you can change those attitudes by excellence, personal gut performance . . . It's a piece of cake until you get to the top. You

find you can't stop playing the game the way you've always played it . . . so you are lean and mean and resourceful and you continue to walk on the edge of the precipice because over the years you have become fascinated by how close to the edge you can walk without losing your balance.

As the four of us walked toward the court house, there was little conversation, but many silent prayers. I thought, *Steve, if you could change all this in one second's time—return to 1973 and have things the way they were and not know the Lord— or be here now, perhaps on the way to prison, but knowing the Lord, which would you choose?*

I would go to prison gladly, if that were a prerequisite for my knowing the Lord. I broke the silence to tell Harvey my thoughts, and she squeezed my hand in agreement.

We recognized several faces as we approached the courtroom. There were people from the State and Federal Securities departments and a man from the Postal Department. The Assistant U.S. Attorney brought her boss. I recalled seeing my name on the indictment: UNITED STATES OF AMERICA vs. STEPHEN P. LAWSON. It appeared that the United States of America was well represented.

Judge Warner* was presiding, a good sign, my attorney thought, in that he was considered one of the more compassionate judges in Atlanta. When my name was called, my attorney asked if people could speak on my behalf, and the judge nodded his permission.

Tim Jones spoke, testifying to our long friendship, the dramatic change in me since I had become a Christian, and asking the judge to be merciful in his decision.

Then Harvey spoke at length, explaining her love for me and at the same time her frustration over what my actions had done to our lives. "I'm the mother of a beautiful five-year-old, and we don't deserve what has happened to us.

We have been publicly ridiculed and have lost all our money. I don't know what Stephen's fate might be, but I know I could leave him and try to make a new life for myself." Then she went on to explain her own conversion to faith in Christ, that both of us were new people, that she had forgiven me for what I had done. She believed I was worthy of her confidence—and the judge's.

After she finished, I spoke for myself for a few minutes. Then my attorney added these words: "Your Honor, Stephen and his wife have been friends of my wife and me for many years. He just got caught up in trying to be successful, because he envied others of his friends who lived on the Northwest side of town."

I could hardly believe my ears. Whose side was he on, anyway? He continued in this vein, and then the Assistant U.S. Attorney spoke, presenting the U.S. government's side quite thoroughly. When she finished we waited for the verdict. Tom had speculated that if I had to serve time it wouldn't exceed six months. Although I hoped for the best, in my heart I knew the roof was about to cave in. For, in truth, had I been the judge and heard what had been presented, I would have given a long, tough sentence.

Without emotion, Judge Warner looked me in the eye and said he was sentencing me to four years on one count of mail fraud and four years on one count of security violations, the time to run consecutively. On the third count he sentenced me to five years of probation, to begin after my prison sentence had been served.

Eight years of confinement! I was so stunned I had to ask my attorney if I had heard correctly. I wasn't the only one taken by surprise; the judge was about to leave the bench when Tom regained the presence of mind to ask the judge to allow me to turn myself in to whatever facility was to be designated, and to allow me forty-five days to get my affairs into order. This was granted.

There was a brief booking downstairs where fingerprints and mug shots were taken, and within half an hour I was free to leave. We shook hands with my attorney and departed, the Lawsons and Joneses, still in shock.

———◆———

Several weeks later I learned that I would go to Eglin Federal prison camp in Ft. Walton Beach, Florida. Just months before a law had been changed, affecting where I could be sent. Previously, anyone with a sentence of five years or longer could not qualify for an "honor camp" but had to do his time in a maximum security "gladiator" camp such as the Atlanta Penitentiary.

Harvey started looking for a job. She needed a good one that would provide a greater salary than any she'd had in the past. Within a few days, she received a job offer with exactly the salary for which we'd been praying. She could start right away, while I was at home, and I could help out while she eased into her new routine.

We worked out a household budget, stripping expenses to cover only the most necessary items. Her new salary would not quite stretch; she would need another three hundred dollars per month.

"That's not too bad, though," I commented. "I'm sure that some of our brothers and sisters in Christ will gladly donate some money each month to your well-being, if I ask." I made a prospective list. If six people gave fifty dollars a month, that would do it.

When the first several people looked me in the eye and said "no," I wasn't discouraged. But the list continued and one "no" followed another.

"Don't feel bad for having asked. I'd do the same thing," one man told me.

"Why don't you sell some of your furniture?" another suggested.

"Why can't Harvey move to a cheaper apartment?" someone else said.

Finally, a brother suffering a sudden attack of wisdom offered the *coup de grace*: "The Lord has told me to tell you that Harvey must live on her salary and make whatever sacrifices she must, to be self-sufficient." In donating his opinion he had named Jesus as an innocent accomplice.

Could this be happening? I was shocked to learn that Christians didn't have the closeness that Jewish people exhibit toward one another at times like these. I hurt badly, not only for my family, but for those in our Christian family who had said "no."

At length I decided to visit Grace Kinser, a dear and wise friend of sixty-plus years who was such an encourager in the faith to Harvey and me. I filled her in on what I'd tried to accomplish in Harvey's behalf. "Grace, can it be that all these people are speaking God's will?" I asked. "Can it be that he wants my family to suffer because I was out of his will? Doesn't he care what will happen to my family?"

I looked up and saw that she was in tears.

"Steve, let's pray for them and forgive them for their actions," she said, softly. After a moment of prayer, she asked for a list of those I'd visited. Very, very reluctantly I gave it to her.

A few days after I left for prison, our friends, including those on my list, arrived at Grace's home for fellowship and refreshments. Then Grace rose and told everyone why she had asked them to meet. She opened her Bible, read several passages, shared her perceptions of Scripture and our family, and then asked how much each would give as a monthly love offering. By evening's end an individual had been appointed to receive the funds and, for the next several months, present a check to Harvey.

This group was augmented by others from the Cathedral of St. Philip who felt it was God's will that they share our financial burden. Only three weeks after my arrival at prison, our friend Bob phoned Harvey. "At this morning's prayer breakfast, we asked for pledges of support and received pledges and checks for more than *four thousand dollars*. People have called my office all day, and the amount has risen to more than *seven thousand!*"

These heartfelt, anonymous gifts gave continual, tangible proof of the love, grace and mercy of God in people's hearts. Their effect on us rose far beyond any dollars-and-cents total.

Thus I learned some vitally important lessons. I learned that I must look ultimately to God, because people will let you down (at least in their initial, human responses). And I must trust *God* to provide for my family. I had meant to see that my family was taken care of—by me.

Many times during those weeks prior to prison, I was asked to witness for Christ. Each of these occasions strengthened me immeasurably. I shall always remember my final evening before departing for prison. I had been invited by Gary Eubanks to speak at the First Baptist Church of Marietta, Georgia. Gary was the attorney who had represented some twenty of my former clients to whom I now owed more than $200,000. He and I still were legal adversaries. But we also were brothers in Christ, and he was bold enough to invite me to speak at his church.

I closed my testimony that night by explaining that I was standing on 1 Peter 5:5-10:

Young men, in the same way be submissive to those who are older. All of you, clothe yourselves with humility toward one another, because "God opposes the proud but gives grace to the humble." Humble yourselves, therefore, under God's mighty hand, that he may lift you up in due time. Cast all your anxiety on him because he cares for you.

Be self-controlled and alert. Your enemy the devil prowls around like a roaring lion looking for someone to devour. Resist him, standing firm in the faith, because you know that your brothers throughout the world are undergoing the same kind of sufferings.

And the God of all grace, who called you to his eternal glory in Christ, after you have suffered a little while, will himself restore you and make you strong, firm and steadfast.

Chapter 15

Family Visit

"It is nonsense to say God fills the gap," Deitrich Bonhoeffer wrote. "He does not fill it, but keeps it empty so that our communion with another may be kept alive, even at the cost of pain. The dearer and richer our memories, the more difficult the separation. From the moment we awake until we fall asleep we must commend our loved ones wholly and unreservedly to God, and leave them in his hands, transforming our anxiety for them into prayers on their behalf."

I had been at Eglin for two weeks and understood the experiences and attitudes that shaped Bonhoeffer's words. Each morning before I arose, I'd pray for Harvey and Blake's well-being. At times I wondered if I had *really* turned them over to God, or if I cared about them as much as I should. Although I felt peaceful, was I really at peace or had my love and caring turned to indifference? Had the miles between us made more of a difference than I cared to admit? Had I become so concerned about myself and my prison life that I felt too little concern for them?

All my life, caring had meant *doing,* or at least worrying. But now, unable to *do* anything, I felt a strange peace; it transcended anything I could conjure up. Further, the more I relied on God, the more he seemed to provide. I began to learn that I couldn't rely on my feelings. I had to concentrate on trusting a God outside of myself and beyond my own powerlessness. And I had to wait and see how life would unfold.

Friday came. Harvey and Blake were driving down from Atlanta and would stay with the Culps that weekend. They'd arrive in Destin early that evening and would meet me in the prison visiting room at nine the next morning.

Though Harvey and I had been married thirteen years, I'd been through several stages of acquiring a new crush on her. I never grew tired of her expressive face and her equally engaging conversation. There was still something about watching her walk into a room that made my heart pound.

Anticipating Harvey's arrival was almost more than I could stand. I acted a lot like a kid on his first date. I got up at the crack of dawn, shaving around my newly acquired beard and getting ready to see her. In my mind, the day had nearly passed by the time I saw their car approaching.

I worried for a moment. How did I look, dressed in my prison outfit, beginning to grow the beard I'd always wanted? What kind of atmosphere would the visiting area offer Blake? Would he be ashamed of me? Perhaps I should have been clean-shaven so my appearance would be the same.

"Stephen Lawson, 07209, you have a visitor," bellowed a voice from the loud speaker. I hurried to the visiting area to meet them. Harvey and Blake did a double take as I walked through the door. The beard, my prison garb, and the loss of about ten pounds somewhat took them aback.

"Daddy!" Blake yelled, running toward me after a tiny hesitation. I picked him up and gave him a long, long hug. Harvey and I embraced.

She had brought a basket full of goodies from home, and we found a table outside and proceeded to unpack her feast. She had even baked brioche for me, a fancy party roll that I particularly liked.

Harvey and I wanted and needed to discuss so many things but could accomplish only a portion of what we'd hoped, as Blake kept running over from the swing area to demand my attention.

It was wonderful, being with Harvey. I could actually lean over and touch her arm. And to hear her reassuring words—that made life worth living, worth getting through my time in this place.

Blake reacted well to this new environment. The place didn't look like a jail. There were no people with guns, no guard towers, bars, or high walls. It matched the description I'd given him the morning I left home . . . "a place where daddies go when they've made mistakes." Indeed, other daddies were there that morning, also many children Blake's age.

It was exhilarating to be a family again, even under our circumstances and for the short time involved. Harvey and I felt God's presence in our daily happenings and efforts, despite our separation. Watching Blake as he played with another inmate's child in the prison yard, we were amazed at how we could experience such normalcy in this difficult atmosphere.

Prior to my leaving, Blake had been accepted into one of Atlanta's excellent private schools. Yet, after my sentencing, we knew that tuition expenses were out of the question. So I was dumbfounded to learn from Harvey that Blake's tuition would be paid by parents of one of his preschool classmates, also accepted at the school, until my return.

"You're joking!" I exclaimed. Who on earth would do such a generous thing? When Harvey told me, I was mystified. I'd never even heard of the people. Harvey had other news, equally moving. Her mother had helped us with carpools and the myriad other jobs that go with assisting a busy working mother and an active small boy. Renee, Harvey's sister, went even further. She leased her furnished home in order to move in with Harvey and help with everything from rent to keeping house. Two magnificent ladies— just like Harvey. I was overwhelmed.

Blake climbed onto my lap. He seemed much heavier than the last time I'd held him. "Daddy?"

"What, Honey?"

"When you came to prison, why did you take all the money with you?"

The innocent question flashed like a bolt of lightning. It was two weeks into the ordeal, and already he was noticing the economic difference. Not only that, he assumed that I was taking the money, rather than realizing that we simply didn't have any.

Harvey and I attempted to explain. It wasn't what we said that helped, I think, but rather that Blake saw his father and mother united on the subject. After our explanation, he smiled. "Okay," he said. "But after you get out of here, will you go to work and help Mommie earn some money? She's working really hard . . ."

Such remarks are a man's real punishment; they go far beyond the judge's intent at the time of sentencing.

Saturday and Sunday sped by. I walked Blake and Harvey to the door and watched as she made several trips to the car, carrying articles from the visiting area. I was not allowed to assist her and hated watching her struggle with heavy items.

When time came to say good-bye, Blake began to cry and begged to stay. I held him for ten minutes, talking to him as I carried him around the visiting area. For each of us, the good-bye was difficult. For days after I felt horrible.

"The first visit's always the hardest," advised a fellow inmate. "Take my word for it, it gets easier. And always remember: the visit's not for you, but for your family. Make sure your spirits are high, so your positive attitude will reinforce theirs." I took that as a direct message from the Lord and tucked it into my heart.

———◆———

For Harvey, the visit was far from over:

As we drove away, I talked calmly to Blake, but inside I panicked. I hadn't thought he would cry so; I hadn't thought I would be so devastated myself. We had been so "up" for the trip, so excited about seeing Stephen. But I wasn't prepared for such a letdown.

"Wasn't it wonderful visiting with Daddy?" I asked Blake.

"Yes, but why can't he come home with us?"

"Daddy will be home someday—soon, I hope—and it will be great to be a family again. Didn't Daddy look different with his beard? Did it tickle when he kissed you?"

Blake started to cry again, and when I couldn't console him with words I pulled the car off the road and cuddled him for a few moments. I prayed, asking God to give us the strength to drive the 350 miles back to Atlanta. I asked for peace for both Blake and me, and courage to make it through the next week.

This was my life now, that of a single parent. It was hard. But it was okay. God was continually faithful to Blake and me. I remembered the last drive like this when it was just Liz and me, after leaving Stephen two weeks before. I had asked the Lord to help me through the next several days. Had it been that long already? We had made it through the first two weeks. The visit with Stephen had been so natural. Maybe, just maybe, Blake and I could make it, after all.

Chapter 16

Invisible Support

On "the outside," I'd attended many prayer group meetings. Yet none could compare with those that met at 4:30 each day at Eglin.

We were prisoners. We had acute, obvious needs to confess and pray about. Unlike those groups at home, ours included men with various backgrounds of education, race, culture, and denomination. Our group changed constantly as some members got released and new members arrived.

At Eglin, as at other prisons, everyone looks the same and no facades are erected to say, "I'm okay." Former politicians, heads of large corporations, and civic leaders mingle their lives with dope pushers and armed robbers. Dressed in hand-me-down Air Force blues and without access to blowdryers for our hair, we looked equally undistinguished and disreputable.

From this group of people, however, emerged several who loved God enough to serve the others, thus assuming some degree of spiritual leadership. Chaplain George Castillo, who headed all religious programs at Eglin, served as our official leader.

Chaplain Castillo was perhaps the hardest working and least appreciated man—by the staff, at least—at Eglin. None of us could fail to appreciate his gracious spirit in that no-win job, caught as he was between inmates and administration.

He had to program a full range of services—Roman Catholic, Protestant, Spanish Mass, Juma prayers, and even time for the Black Awareness Choir to rehearse. Then there was the Chapel Choir, responsibility for driving Jewish inmates to services held on the Air Force base, plus the Bible study programs scheduled in the evenings when people from the First Baptist Church of Fort Walton Beach would come in to teach.

Our prayer group learned about faith in action. As prisoners we soon learned we could change very little about our lives. We were told when to eat, sleep, and work. At home, for example, if my wife phoned to say the air conditioner wouldn't work, I'd take care of it. In prison we could do almost nothing about what happened at home—except pray. In that stark setting, I learned much about effective prayer.

We prayed for one another. Some men entered the group in the lowest of emotional states. For them, the Lord provided special strength and encouragement. Others had not yet recognized their need for Jesus because they had never faced up to their own desperation. Although impregnated with disillusionment, they came to meet God. We learned that Jesus could and would meet us at our point of need.

We kept a simple format: thirty minutes devoted to conversation and listing prayer requests, followed by thirty minutes of prayer. Our talk wasn't always spiritual; often it centered around secular events and our personal frustrations. Sometimes I attended more out of duty than anything else.

Despite our emotional and spiritual limitations, we began to love one another. A bond developed among us; we became soul mates. It's impossible to live with people—share their spiritual peaks and valleys, their intimate dreams, and fervently pray for them in the group and individually—without growing very close. We came to know one another's families because we prayed for them so often.

"How's Jane's back doing?" we'd ask, as though we were well acquainted with Jane, although we had never met her.

Our "group" at first numbered three or four, then included as many as forty. At first I assumed they'd all had pretty much the same sort of spiritual experiences as I'd had, but that wasn't the case.

A person comes in contact with real characters in such a setting, people who would look unbelievable in any other place. Such a person was Joe, "The Butcher."

Joe had served about eight years at the Atlanta Federal Penitentiary before coming to Eglin. That in itself is rather unusual because the Atlanta Pen is where the most hard-core criminals are warehoused. People at the Atlanta Pen *never* left, because a guy with only a twenty-year stint was considered a short timer. Not only that, the Atlanta Pen was a maximum-security prison, whereas Eglin was far from that. If you wanted to escape from Eglin all you had to do was call a cab and sneak over the white line that was painted on the cement to indicate the point over which inmates were not allowed to pass. Many people have said that a place like Eglin is a much tougher place to do time than at one of the real joints, as they are called. Being almost free is very hard on a man, where if you are really "locked down" it is easier to come to grips with your situation.

Joe had been one of the short timers at the Atlanta Pen, as he had only a sixteen-year sentence. What he did and what he actually got caught doing isn't my story to relate. The truth is that The Butcher often said he wished he was able to give his complete story and witness to God's work in his life, but that some of the things he had been involved with had no statute of limitations. So I never pressed, and he never offered more than a few snatches. Reportedly, he was a Mafia chieftain. He certainly looked the part; at fifty-three years of age he was about five-feet-five and weighed about two hundred and thirty pounds of solid muscle. He used to bench-press four hundred and fifty pounds but claimed that, since he was older and the sun was so hot in the middle of summer, he had tapered down to just three-fifty or three-seventy-five.

I vividly remember Joe's first couple of days at Eglin. He is the type of guy who never met a stranger in his life. Aside from that, I'm fairly confident that his coming was known and quietly publicized, because as soon as he set foot on the compound, every Italian was there to welcome him. It was something you had to see to believe. Anywhere he walked he was followed by as many as ten to twenty inmates. If he said hello to a person, *everyone* said hello in return. If he told a joke, everyone laughed. And other people's jokes were considered funny only if The Butcher laughed at them.

One of those first days The Butcher and his Armada came sailing down the sidewalk. I said hello and nodded but received no response. (I later found out he was practically blind without glasses and merely hadn't seen me.) Another day the group passed me again, and I ventured to say, "How's it going?" The Butcher stared at me and said, "Okay, okay." I was so amazed that this bigshot had spoken to me that I responded, kindly, of course, "Well, praise God."

At that point The Butcher stopped in his tracks and wheeled around, a big grin on his face. "Yeah, yeah, praise the Lord, Brother. You know the Lord? Yeah? Good! Nice to meet you, Brother, What's your name? Steve Lawson, huh? I'll try to remember, but I'm not too good with names, you know what I mean?"

All this time he was shaking my hand, and the pain from his grip shot almost up to my armpit.

"Listen, Lawson, you come to The Butcher's cube. We'll talk some. I got some fruit in. You like peaches?"

With that, the group continued on their way, but I noticed that they smiled to me and let me know that I had passed some kind of test. That evening I looked up The Butcher in his cube. After all, he had extended an invitation, and it certainly wouldn't be wise to run the risk of offending or insulting him.

As I approached his cube, it appeared as though "Little Italy" was having a block party. In the middle of all the people The Butcher was holding court. When our eyes met, he sprang into action. "Okay, youse guys, clear out. I got company. Come in, come in."

He asked me my name again, and I told him, and invited him to call me Steve.

"The name's Joe 'The Butcher.' Call me anything you like. Most people just call me Joe or refer to me as The Butcher. Take a peach for yourself. They're in my locker."

"No, thanks. I'm not hungry."

"I said, take a peach," The Butcher stated. "What do I have to do—break your arm?"

"As a matter of fact, I'd love a peach," I replied.

We settled back and talked. There was an unmistakable charm about this hulk of a man, and when you looked into his eyes or when he grinned, Jesus was all over his face. We were to see each other daily at prayer group. However, I would be tested for several months before being totally accepted—because I wasn't Italian.

"Mama mia," he would say. "What am I going to do with you?"

The second thing to overcome with The Butcher was that I was in Eglin for a white-collar crime. He said that guys like me were phonies because we had to rob people with a pen; we didn't have the courage to put a gun in their faces. He also said that my pen was more lethal than his gun, anyway. To hear The Butcher talk, vice could almost sound like virtue as long as it was done out in the open, above board—*and* you were Italian.

The Butcher became the object of daily prayer in our prison fellowship group. He had been in front of the Parole Board on several occasions, and each time they had said they weren't ready to review his case and asked him to come back in twenty-four months. In another four or five months he was scheduled to see the Board again.

All the time Joe was at Eglin he was a visible part of that compound. He had become a Christian at the Atlanta Pen. He read the Word every morning. Any time you visited his cube the Bible was open to a new section. His ministry was to those younger men who felt too big for their own good. He was "Mister Crime," and his words carried a lot of authority.

"Listen, Jesus was no punk," he would explain. "He could have copped out any time he wanted to but he never did, and he never ratted out his friends. He was a stand-up guy."

It's amazing to realize how many different—yet effective—parts of the body Jesus has. Joe was, and is to this day I'm sure, a "stand-up guy" for the Lord he loves. Christ put an undeniable burden on my heart to write a letter on his behalf to the Parole Board. The hour before he was to meet them Joe prayed and then went back to his cube and fell asleep.

"What do I have to worry about?" he said. "Jesus is here with me, and I just show up to see what is going on."

Incredibly, he was told that in four short months he would be free to go home.

I missed The Butcher after he left. Aside from the fellowship we shared, I wasn't able to get any good fruit!

Unquestionably, many inmates were drawn to our prayer fellowship group initially to see what Joe The Butcher was doing there. No one ever criticized him as he ordered other brothers to pray or as he launched into prayer himself, sounding somewhat like a motor boat pulling away from the dock.

We saw fascinating miracles. Orlando Cepeda, for example. I'll always remember his large, dark eyes and the pain they revealed. Others know Orlando as a star baseball player with the St. Louis Cardinals (where he was named Most Valuable Player in the National League one year) or with the Atlanta Braves or Boston Red Sox teams somewhat later. We prayed regularly for Orlando's family, but especially for his mother, who took his incarceration very hard. Though Orlando expected to be released soon, his mother was falling into deeper and deeper depression. One week Orlando came into the prayer group, sat down, and wept like a baby. His mother's depression had worsened to the point that she could no longer care for herself. She was to be committed to a public mental institution in Puerto Rico the next afternoon. We asked Orlando if we could lay hands on him and pray in proxy for his mother, and he agreed.

Five of us prayed with all our hearts for Orlando's mother to be healed instantly. When our prayer concluded, I suddenly acquired the worst headache of my life. My hands began to sweat. I figured that Satan must have gone to work, that a miracle was in process and he couldn't stand it. As I prayed aloud for Jesus to heal my hurting head, other brothers laid hands on me with prayer and bound Satan in the name of Jesus.

My head started to feel better, and I glanced at Orlando. He was still in tears. I had never been especially sensitive in discerning spirits, but I found myself walking over to him.

"Orlando, do you feel that your mother's problems have been caused by you? Do you feel guilty or unworthy?"

"Yes," he said through tears. "I know I have been a good son to her, but I can't help feeling personally responsible for what is happening." With that we prayed for Orlando again, asking Jesus to free him from the false spirits of guilt, condemnation, and unworthiness. Orlando was at last delivered from this torment. We could see the tranquility transform his face and relax his body. The Lord had sent the Comforter, who had taken control.

At our prayer group meeting the next day, Orlando could hardly wait to speak. "Last night my wife went to my mother's apartment to help her pack for the institution. She opened the door and found my mother as lucid as all of us in this room."

A murmur of "Praise the Lord" went around our circle. The Butcher's voice was no murmur; from him came a "Thank you, Jesus!" that rocked the room.

"I asked my wife when this happened," Orlando continued. "Figuring the time change between here and Puerto Rico, it had to be *the very time* we prayed for her."

Chuck*, another sweet-spirited fellow, came into our prayer group through "divine accident." Returning to my barracks one afternoon, I saw this nice-looking young man I recognized as new in the facility. He looked sad and completely alone. I introduced myself, and soon we were talking.

In the course of our talk, I shared with him about Jesus. And, amazingly enough, by the end of our conversation, Chuck had invited Christ into his life.

Secretly, I was extremely proud of myself. After all, I had obeyed the call of God's Spirit and made myself available to Chuck. Not only that, but look how well I'd directed the conversation! I came to the conclusion that I had helped "close the deal" for the Lord.

Then Chuck burst my bubble. "I can't wait to phone my mother," he exclaimed. "My whole life will be different now. Mom's a Christian. She has prayed for my salvation every day for the past twenty years."

I felt very foolish. I had been ready to take credit for this conversion, having spent an hour of my time with Chuck. He went on to say that his brother and sister-in-law had talked with him about faith in Christ numerous times since they had become Christians six years ago.

I left Chuck, returned to my cube, and opened the Bible. I read of Jesus riding into Jerusalem on a donkey. People lining the streets applauded and waved palm branches. I thought of my conversation with Chuck and smiled to myself. *Boy, if that donkey thought the applause was for him . . . !*

Life with the prayer group continued on a day-to-day, crisis-to-crisis basis. One of the brothers learned his wife had been raped by a motorcycle gang. Another man lost two children in an accident. Some men learned their wives were unfaithful; others found themselves faced with divorce proceedings.

Those troubles were real and affected us all. When the group got to a low ebb, however, you could count on The Butcher to stand up and tell the guys what babies they were. He knew how to snap people out of their pity parties:

"Youse guys wouldn't make it for a week in Atlanta. You have it so good here you can't imagine, and you walk around with your heads down. Fine examples you set for your families. They're the ones who have it rough. You know you're gonna be fed, have clean sheets on the bed. You don't have a problem in the world. Your wives probably don't have enough money to get along, have to work full-time and take care of the kids. Then what happens? Mama mia, you get on the phone sounding depressed and drive them crazy! What does The Butcher have to do, rap you on the side of the head?"

Our periods of learning were made up of tears, laughter, depression, joy, but through it all, growth. We always agreed, despite our differences, when it came to praying for a child. As a group, we adopted several children. Our hearts went out to one child in particular.

Can you imagine being in prison and learning that your three-year-old son was dying of cancer? That man felt so helpless and suffered such despair that without the fellowship of Christ, there's no telling what he would have done.

Our prison fellowship prayer group contacted the warden and insisted that he call Washington to obtain furlough privileges for a father whose baby was given only three months to live. The prayers that went up for that family! The superintendent worked with the parole board in Washington to get that father an early release.

Our brother left us, but we continued to pray for God to heal that little boy. His dad was home for four months prior to Jesus taking the child home. He wrote to describe the final weeks, a letter that tore us apart.

Praying for that child for over a year unified the prayer group, and his death was devastating to us, especially those who were new in the Lord. We'd prayed for a miracle, however, and I had to believe that God heard and answered. Our brother had begun to reconstruct his life at home. And his last letter brought news that they were expecting a baby.

———◆———

While I was at Eglin, my mother died.

Though her health had been failing for many years, it was hard to imagine that her life could stop. She had been a fighter, wrestling with life every day, from the time I'd known her. And life had been so difficult for Mother—from poor to rich to poor again, loss of her friends, hopes, and dreams.

Her last will and testament stated that she was to be cremated and her ashes spread over the ocean. She especially requested that there be no funeral services. This made sense; Mother had alienated most of the important people in her life. In spreading her ashes she obviated having to be buried next to Dad—a man she never forgave. *Gritty to the end, weren't you, Mother?* I thought, marveling at the toughness of this tiny lady who'd continually been my adversary—and my mother.

When I told my case manager about Mother's death and requested time to be with my family, he had to turn me down. "I spoke to the people in administration," he told me, "and they said, 'no funeral, no furlough.'"

"You mean that if Mother had decided to have a funeral I would have been allowed a five-day furlough, yet since she didn't, I don't get any leave at all?"

"That's about it. Bureau of Prison policy," he replied.

Mother willed her entire estate to Rosemary. Her legacy to me took the form of intangibles, some good, some bad. People say I inherited her sense of humor, for which I'm grateful. She was one of the funniest, most charming and gracious hostesses I've known. When her mood was up, she was a joy. But when it was foul . . . well, she wasn't known as the War Empress for nothing. Another thing she had left me was the approach to life that helped me get into prison: "Remember, Steve, a buck is your best friend." Mother and I had shared several negative qualities, including the ability to carry a grudge indefinitely.

In a few days we would celebrate Easter. Emotions ran in extremes in our prayer group. For some, the separation from family was nearly unbearable. For others, it was a high time; we looked forward to the sunrise service we had received permission to conduct. Chaplain Castillo would meet us on the sand behind the dorm buildings and lead us in a worship service as the sun rose.

I had decided not to mention anything to the group about Mother's passing or the institution's decision not to permit me to be with my family at this time. I was afraid it would only be opportunity for bitterness and anger, thus dampening the joy and holiness of Easter Sunday.

After that Sunday, though, Harvey told me over the phone that it was important for me to commend Mother's spirit to God in prayer. I didn't understand what that meant—I'm still not sure what it means—but I did as she suggested. In prayer, I committed Mother's spirit into God's keeping, expressing hope that she and Dad could have eternal life in heaven.

It is useless to theologize on this point. To my knowledge, neither of my parents ever came to a faith in Christ. But God granted me peace that day, and how God deals with the souls of other people isn't up to me. Once again, I was powerless and even more aware of how everything ultimately comes from the Lord's hand.

Dr. James Monroe, pastor of the First Baptist Church of Fort Walton Beach, often visited our group. Dr. Monroe is a man who loves God, and he loved each of us; in fact, his church adopted us. Dr. Monroe arranged for baptismal candidates from the prison to receive a believer's baptism at his church. He held revival services in the prison for a week each year, showed us slides from his most recent trip to the Holy Land, and sent a stream of wonderful musicians and Bible teachers to encourage and train us as Christians.

In turn, Dr. Monroe often arranged to transport us to First Baptist, where our prison fellowship choir would sing and give testimonies. Then there would be fellowship, homemade food cooked by the ladies, and the warmth that comes from being received into the body of Christ and made welcome.

Like the other inmates, I received several unforgettable blessings from God during my prison term. But knowing and loving that godly servant heads the list.

Loving, serving, praying, forgiving, learning . . . what lessons that motley group of men were to experience together! Sometimes even now, I think of those times, thank God once again, and pray for brothers incarcerated at Eglin whom I've never known.

There we all learned that the Lord's grace abounds even in one of Satan's prime breeding grounds: America's prisons.

Chapter 17

Crisis in Springfield

During the twenty-minute ride to the airport, my pain became unbearable. I asked for and received permission to lie down in the rear of the empty prison station wagon. An inmate driver and the prison doctor, beside him on the front seat, were taking me to a private airport.

The "Doc" (actually a physician's assistant) was convinced that I had medical problems beyond his scope. Just what his scope was, none of us knew. The story had been circulated that he had once treated an inmate for jaundice for three months before noticing that the man was Chinese. He even had problems keeping potted plants alive in the infirmary. Actually, the doctor's poor attitude accomplished a great deal in terms of preventative medicine; five hundred inmates were scared to death of getting sick. But my X-rays had shown that the neck and arm pains I suffered were not merely subjective. I'd have to transfer to Springfield Prison for treatment.

Since some airlines were striking, the prison had chartered a private plane to transport me. Had they not considered this trip an emergency, I'd have taken a series of prison planes and buses, shackled the entire way. I was grateful to miss that experience, as well as the series of jails in which I would have been held pending various connections.

When we landed, we discovered there was no guard waiting to escort me to the prison. Since the pilot needed to return to Florida without delay, I found myself in the strange position of bidding him farewell and phoning the prison for instructions.

"Steve who?" someone asked. "What are you talking about?" It seemed that a week earlier, "Doc" had requested that I be accepted for possible surgery; the request had been approved, but my arrival date had never been confirmed. I explained that the pilot had left me at the airport and jokingly mentioned that unless they picked me up I'd be willing to fly to Mexico for the winter, since Eglin didn't expect me back for a while. My humor was appreciated, but they assured me a guard would be on the way.

The guard was the tight-lipped type. I attempted to ask a few questions. "Would you say I have anything to fear pertaining to my personal safety here?"

"Just keep your nose clean," he replied. "Everything will be okay." For some reason I didn't feel reassured.

Springfield Prison appeared over the knoll of a nearby hill, and its very appearance confirmed every horrible thing I'd heard about the place the past few weeks. Towers that housed armed guards rose ominously to the forefront. The entire place was bordered by a high brick wall with double rows of barbed wire as added security.

First I was taken to the receiving room, where I was strip searched, given new prison clothing, then pushed into a holding cell. There I waited while they readmitted an inmate who several weeks earlier had attempted to commit suicide by swallowing lye. They had taken him to a local hospital, and he was returning with tubes still protruding from his stomach.

From the opposite direction came a stretcher holding the body of an inmate who had recently expired. A blanket covered his face, and the guards ignored everything about the body except for papers that had to be filled out.

Next came a busload of shackled prisoners who arrived from other facilities. They were processed—searched, photographed—while I waited.

I asked the guard if he would hand me my Bible through the bars, but he refused, claiming that it hadn't been examined yet, and told me I needed to be quiet and not hassle anyone.

Soon they assigned me to a building, floor, and hospital bed, and I was escorted to my new home. Portions of the prison housed up to three hundred occupants at any time—incorrigibles who came from prisons around the country. Many could not be handled by their guards, so they had been sent there to be segregated and placed under Thorozine to calm them.

The rest of the population numbered about five hundred and were mostly transients. We came from other prisons, and were there for medical and/or psychological problems—some real, some imagined. Certain inmates from Marion Prison, for example, said they'd been there for ten years and wanted a change of scenery. Feigning back problems allowed them to leave long enough to catch at least a glimpse of some late-model cars and see how the world had changed.

That evening I phoned home after waiting in line for the single available pay phone for more than two hours, to tell my concerned wife that everything looked fine and she was not to worry. I sounded more convinced of that than I actually felt.

Bizarre experiences and characters awaited me at this place. The second evening in my new home I walked in on a rape when I entered the showers; I exited quickly. I soon learned that no one got underneath his covers in bed without untucking both sides. That way you could escape an attack from either side without delay.

The fellow in the bed next to mine had pornographic tattoos all over his body, "Love" and "Hate" tattooed on the fingers of each hand, and a red and purple likeness of a devil that curled from the muscle on his left arm down to a point on the back of his hand. He wore mirrored sunglasses at all times.

"You a preacher?" he asked, taking note of my Bible.

"No," I answered, launching him into a long, hostile monologue wherein this roommate proceeded to tell me about his plans to escape, catch his wife and her lover, tie them up, and douse them with gasoline. He described how he'd laugh as they burned to a crisp. A Bible placed in his room during a stay in solitary confinement had been his only diversion, and he had asked Christ into his life. After his release from solitary, he had committed his fifth murder; he now considered himself a Christian murderer.

Nobody was in a hurry here. It took me five days to see a doctor, and they took their time administering a series of tests. Eventually my treatment included traction for several days and instructions to return to Eglin, with directions not to lift anything heavier than twenty-five pounds. My weight was heading down to 148 pounds, significantly less than the 182 I'd carried on my six-foot-one frame when I first entered Eglin.

I heard that they had fresh eggs on the menu that first Sunday and made sure I found the mess hall. It took twenty minutes to reach the head of the line, and as I headed toward a table a hand came from nowhere, took my plate off the tray, dumped its contents onto another plate, then put my empty plate back on its tray. Startled, I looked up at the man who belonged to the hand. He must have been six-foot-five, with the arms of a sumo wrestler. I simply smiled and said that I hoped he would enjoy his eggs.

I looked around the mess hall as I ate my toast and drank the C-ration coffee. My eyes settled at last on a figure I can only describe as a walking nut factory—The General.

He stood at attention, his eyes straight ahead, his tray held chest high. As the line moved ahead he took the smartest of military steps forward. At the steam line, he saluted the inmates behind the counter. All eyes in the place were riveted on him as he left the line and looked for a place to sit.

He crossed the huge room and marched directly to my table. He came to a halt, clicked his heels twice, and motioned with his head toward an empty chair opposite me. He didn't say a word.

"Sure, sit down. It's not taken," I said. He sat with his back erect and began to eat a "square meal." Any military school graduate can tell you about a "square meal": bring food straight up from your plate to mouth height, then straight across to your mouth, then reverse the process to return the fork to the plate. The face looks forward with eyes straight ahead, never looking to the left or right.

All this The General did, but with one interesting variation; he didn't use any eating utensils. Egg yolk dripped between his fingers, and he seemed oblivious to all that surrounded him. "Excuse me," I said, departing in haste. Apparently he didn't hear me.

The next time I went to the mess hall, The General showed up again. I watched him salute the people along the wall. As he marched through the line, something told me he'd present himself at my table. Sure enough, he zig-zagged his way past hundreds of others, crossed the room, and searched out the far corner where I sat. Again, the head motion toward the empty seat, the repeated heel clicking. I nodded okay, and he sat down.

This time the "square meal" business involved spaghetti and meat sauce—with his fingers, of course, putting yesterday's egg exhibition to shame. Soon meat sauce covered his face, hands, shirt, and half the table. His head wasn't in much better shape as he'd run his fingers through his hair in an attempt to keep it out of his face.

I decided I wouldn't leave this time. Nothing, including The General's insanity, would prevent me from eating my Italian cuisine. Doubtless the General couldn't understand a word I'd say, which gave me courage to speak. "General, someday I'd like to invite you to my mother-in-law's house for dinner. I know Marjory would love to meet you. I'll tell her about you, but I know she won't believe me."

The General paid no attention whatever. "You know, General," I continued, "I'm a Christian. And the Lord says in his Word that if we do a good turn for the least of his people, we have done it for him. It seems that you almost qualify as one of his 'least.' I know God loves you and I do, too, but you're a disaster around spaghetti!" I bade The General good-bye and left the table, but he didn't seem to notice.

The same thing happened the next day, though I'd changed locations. "General," I said, "we really have to stop meeting this way. I think my wife is on to us." There was no response from his side of the table, but it didn't matter. I was playing the scene for my own entertainment. When I excused myself from the table I received a sloppy salute from a hand garnished with meat sauce and Thousand Island dressing. The thought crossed my mind that it looked as though the inmates had taken over the asylum.

I returned to my section, lay on the bed, and began reading my Bible. This brought some comments, as usual: "How come you're a Christian, yet you're in here with the rest of us?" I was getting used to that question.

Several yards away, some inmates stood around the bed of a garrulous old-timer who loved to spin a yarn. Usually I paid no attention to their conversation, but today I heard my name. My ears perked up. Most of what they were saying about me was not complimentary. Some of them agreed that jailhouse religion indicated weakness in a man. After all, I had gotten myself into trouble. Why wasn't I man enough to get myself out of trouble without asking God to do it for me? Obviously, my continual Bible reading bugged them.

The old-timer took a different attitude, though. He believed religion was okay, and that if a person wanted it, and it helped him "do time" easier, then that was all right. Then he said the saddest thing I'd ever heard:

"You know, I'm sixty-three years old and don't think I ever had someone pray for *me*."

Without thinking, I got out of bed and walked toward the semi-hostile gathering. I passed the others and stood directly in front of the old-timer. "I heard what you just said and want you to know I'll pray for you right now," I offered.

He began to cry. The crowd instantly dispersed, leaving us alone. I asked the old inmate to name his needs and requests, and after that brief checklist began to pray. Our prayer was intense, earnest, and unrestrained. The Holy Spirit seemed to permeate the whole room. The man was eager to ask Jesus into his life.

Later that evening, another fellow came by. He must have been six-foot-five, and I recognized the arms of the man who'd taken the eggs off my plate that first day in the mess hall. He had moved into our section several days earlier, and he didn't appear to be Jesus' biggest fan, judging from his vocabulary.

This mountain of a fellow acted nervous. He shifted his weight from one foot to the other. "Uh, Preacher, will you, uh—I mean—will you pray for me?"

"Of course I will." I asked him his name.

"It's Larry*." As we held hands and prayed, tears streamed down his face.

"Do you know who Jesus is, Larry?"

"Yes, he's God's Son."

"Is there any reason you shouldn't ask him into your life right now?"

"I dunno."

"Let's pray again, but this time after I get through saying a prayer, I want you to repeat some words after I say them. Okay?"

"Okay, Preacher."

A few minutes later Larry had become my brother in Christ. We found a *Good News for Modern Man* version of the Bible in a magazine rack, and Larry read it faithfully. He had a true hunger for spiritual food. I prayed for Larry for some time.

When my mylogram tests showed that I didn't need surgery, I was assigned to another wing. The guys gave me a brief wave and a "Good-bye, Preacher." I never saw any of them again.

That evening I walked to the mess hall from a different direction than usual, and at a later time. Upon entering the line I saw The General already seated. *It's one thing for him to pick me out*, I thought. *No one can blame me for that. But if I pick him out to sit with, everyone will believe I'm as crazy as he is!* I sat by myself some twenty tables away.

Suddenly The General rose to his feet, picked up his tray, and with great military bearing, came to my table. Our meal went quietly, but he spread dinner all over the place. I couldn't tell if he had an itch or was trying to stuff tuna casserole up his nose.

I returned to my new quarters, glad I could get out of this crazy house, no matter what sort of transportation the Bureau of Prisons provided. That evening, however, I discovered that my urine was red as wine. It was similar to times before when I had passed kidney stones. But I'd never had this much bleeding.

What if jouncing about on the prison bus caused the stone to start moving? I could imagine being in incredible pain, with no access to medical attention and in the company of disinterested and unsympathetic guards. That evening I placed an emergency request to see the doctor.

The next day, x-rays showed nothing. The day after that, the doctor scheduled another test. I was told that since I was over forty years old and nothing had shown up on the x-rays, there was a 40 percent certainty that I'd developed bladder cancer.

That night at dinner I hardly ate at all. The General sat there, eating with that distinctive two-fisted style of his, and I related my despair about the possiblity of discovering bladder cancer in a place like this prison. I expected no loving bedside manner here, of course. The General apparently heard none of my remarks, though he saluted me occasionally.

In bed that evening, the tears flowed. A yard light sent a beam through the barred window, and illuminated my pictures of Blake and Harvey. I prayed like I never had before. I did not want to die.

First, I begged God to spare my life. My prayers did not result in peace, however. Next, I tried to arouse God's sympathies. "Lord, I want Harvey to have the sort of life she deserves. We're a Christian family now, so please add years to my life as you did with Hezekiah, so Harvey and I might grow old together." I mentioned my little boy, and how I wanted to do the things with him my father had never taken the time to do with me.

But the torment continued, with no peace in sight. At three in the morning my pillow was drenched with tears. I had been at it since ten in the evening. Finally, out of sheer exhaustion, I gave up. "Lord, I hoped you wanted me to live a long life. If so, I'm yours and I'll witness to your glory until the day you take me home. But if you want me here for just a short lifetime, I'm still yours. With your help I'll witness, despite illness or pain."

With that, peace came, and I fell asleep immediately.

The next morning when I awoke I was convinced that everything was fine. I felt so refreshed and joyous that I asked God to confirm these feelings if they truly were from him. An inmate wearing surgical greens and a mask came for me with a gurney. He was calling in a Cuban accent: "Praise de Lord! Praise de Lord, where is brother Lawson?"

"Over here!" I half shouted.

"Praise de Lord! He is so faithful!" he chirped. "Don't worry, Brother Lawson. The Lord has a lot of plans for you."

We prayed there in the hall. I knew that God had sent this angel to minister especially to me.

In surgery, the problem turned out to be a kidney stone, after all; it was retrieved with little difficulty. The stone simply hadn't shown up in the x-ray.

That afternoon I explained to the warden that slow prison transportation might cause me to miss my Parole Board meeting that was coming up at Eglin. Within hours, what I consider another miracle occurred: I was given permission to travel from Springfield the next afternoon via commercial bus to Eglin.

Dinner that evening was considerably better than the night before. I was bursting with the good occurrences of the last twenty-four hours, but I had learned that it's wise not to share such things in prison. Others either aren't interested or could be envious of your good fortune. However, I had the perfect dinner companion, one with whom I could share my good news. The General, as usual, didn't get envious or make any comments. I could tell him anything I liked. When he crossed the room to sit with me, I smiled.

"By all means, General," I encouraged. Soon our usual one-way conversation had begun. "Well, General, this is our last dinner. Tomorrow I leave this zoo and return to Eglin."

At that, the General looked directly at me and said, "I'm sorry to hear that. You've been a wonderful sport to put up with all my crap, and I apologize if I've turned your stomach."

I was in shock. The General continued to eat his square meal for the benefit of others sitting around us.

"Do you mean to tell me you're not crazy?" I asked.

"Of course not. Actually, you're more nuts than I am. Why would you sit with someone like me and continually converse with someone who'd never answer you?"

"General, you have a point there, although it's a little late to bring any sort of logic to our relationship. Tell me, though, why do you do all this, anyway?"

He told me he'd graduated from a well-known school of finance, then enlisted in the Marines. "The government wants me on about one hundred and five counts," he said, "and I'm trying to convince everyone I'm spaced out due to battle fatigue."

"Hey, that's your business," I told him. "I wish you all the luck in the world. But you must be stone crazy to have pulled this over on me, night after night."

"I'll miss you," he answered. With that he saluted me, scooped up his mashed potatoes, combed them through his hair, and gave me another three rapid salutes.

When I returned to my section I received the message to report to the clothing room immediately. It was time to be outfitted for my civilian return to Eglin. I was given black socks and shoes, undershorts and tee shirt. Then, in a flash of warped humor, the guard reached for a lime green polyester leisure suit, with a royal blue shirt featuring a print of lime green palm trees. He handed it to me straight-faced. Maybe he *didn't* have a sense of humor, after all. No, I could not make another selection. I was in prison, he informed me. And if I didn't like the way things were done, I should have thought of that before I committed my crime.

The next day I was given a ride to the bus depot. Though I looked disreputable, I was a "free" man for the duration of this trip. No guards or shackles. Just another traveler with very bad taste in clothing.

Springfield had been quite an excursion. I had spent a lot of time reading the Bible—up to ten hours some days. I had encountered some strange people and seen God's grace touch a couple of lives.

But, most importantly, I had entered yet another dimension in Christ. I had faced the possibility of cancer and death and learned to yield even that to God's hands. I would never forget that all-night vigil of prayer and struggle. God had managed to bring me new growth there in the maximum security prison of Springfield.

Chapter 18

Man's Law, God's Grace

I had ignored the Parole Board for quite some time because I had received a "regular adult" sentence. Called an "A" type sentence, it dictated that I'd stay under the judge's authority and *must* serve at least one third of my sentence before parole consideration. This meant that I had to serve at least thirty-two months before becoming eligible for Parole Board consideration or even to be eligible for a furlough.

Soon after I reported to Eglin, my attorneys, who believed my sentence excessive for a white-collar, nonviolent crime, submitted a Rule 35 to Judge Warner. This rule allows a judge to reconsider a sentence upon receipt of new information. It seemed to me that most inmates applied for a Rule 35, as most believed they'd been unfairly sentenced and sought reduced sentences. I believed that a judge knew the facts before he passed a sentence and was therefore unlikely to change his mind.

Despite my intellectual reasoning, I had high hopes. I had read newspaper accounts of seven-year and eight-year sentences being handed down for such heinous crimes as rape and murder. Harvey had asked our friends in the Christian community to write to the judge on my behalf.

There was no new information in my case for the judge to consider. Nevertheless, we submitted the Rule 35 with the hope—certainly not the expectation—that he might change the sentence.

Miraculously, he did just that. Judge Warner did not change the eight-year factor, but he did designate my sentence as B-2, instead of regular adult, which meant that I could see the Parole Board at any time and, should they see fit, serve less than the mandatory sentence less time off for good behavior. Harvey and I rejoiced at this. The judge's action implied that he might have leveled too harsh a sentence after all. Surely the Parole Board would notice that.

I informed my case worker that I'd like to see the Parole Board on their next visit. That appeared to be impossible, since they already had a full schedule. I would have to wait for their next visit in another two months. Meanwhile, I could visit the law library and learn how I could best represent myself. Though my attorney had offered to represent me at that hearing, I wanted to speak to the board myself.

In the course of my research, I discovered a number of factors in my favor:

1. I had made restitution to many of my former clients. I had paid them back as well as given them a 40-percent profit.
2. I voluntarily separated myself from the crime by calling it to the government's attention.
3. I saved the government considerable expense by pleading guilty, rather than prolonging the trial procedure.
4. There were special considerations, too. Blake was feeling the effects of my absence, and we would submit a psychologist's report to that effect. Harvey was encountering financial hardships. Also, I had docu-

mented proof that my back condition required a physician's care.

5. I was not the same man who committed the crimes. I was truly repentant for my past.

6. The institutional adjustment report from my case worker was favorable, recommending that I be granted positive parole consideration.

I readied myself in every way possible for meeting the Parole Board. Our prayer group prayed for me daily. I continued reading the Bible and praying.

I entered the hearing room that day, feeling thankful already. This time I would argue my case myself, rather than have lawyers represent me. My version had never been given clearly in court since I had pleaded guilty.

Two parole board members sat behind a long table, with my case worker positioned to the side. They clicked on a tape recorder, then read a litany of the original proceedings. At last they began questioning me directly, and from the tone of their queries, I could tell they were uninformed about my case. My heart began to sink as I tried to clarify certain aspects of their questions. After a while I was given opportunity to speak. I reviewed all the points I'd listed before, all that seemed favorable to my case. I ended by stating that I was a new person in Jesus Christ, truly repentant, and that the past eight months at Eglin had been used profitably in growing in my Christian faith through reading the Word of God. By the end of my discourse I had begun to weep.

Without changing expression, the Board asked me to wait in the hall while they deliberated. I was nervous but prayerfully confident; I felt sure that the Holy Spirit had given me the right words to say.

Back inside, I was told: "Mr. Lawson, we reviewed the circumstances of your crimes and balanced them against the things you said today. We reviewed your institutional report, which is quite good. The aggravating aspect of your crimes, however, is that you signed a consent decree in 1974 and violated that court order by breaking the security laws again. Therefore, we recommend that you serve sixty-four months."

It took me only a moment to compute this. "That's my eight-year sentence, less time off for good behavior, isn't it?"

"Yes, it is. Do you have any other questions, Mr. Lawson?"

"No, I don't. I guess I'll just have to depend on the Lord to somehow make each of those months a blessing."

"Well, good luck to you. That will be all."

I left the building nauseated and in a state of shock. How could I phone Harvey and tell her I'd remain in prison for more than five additional years? How do you tell a six-year-old that you'll be coming home . . . when he's eleven?

In the chapel, I shared this news with Bill Bevers,* the chaplain's clerk. Bill loved God's Word and could recall it when a person needed it most. And he ministered to me with gentle, caring words and comforting Scriptures that restored my battered spirit.

Scriptures like Ephesians 6:12: "For our struggle is not against flesh and blood, but against the rulers, against the authorities, against the powers of this dark world and against the spiritual forces of evil in the heavenly realms." If so, then what had happened? We knew it wasn't the Lord's will for me to remain in prison sixty-four months.

You may be thinking, *Why not?* Simply, I *knew* that God did not want me there. There was a quiet confidence of that deep in my spirit.

Other Scriptures came to mind then: "And we know that in all things God works for the good of those who love him who have been called according to his purpose" (Romans 8:28). And Hebrews 13:5: "Never will I leave you; never will I forsake you."

Bill helped me to pray for God's peace, for the assurance that God was still in control of my life, and for blessings on Harvey and Blake—and preparation for Harvey to receive this news.

Harvey's reaction was evidence of God's intervention. "Praise the Lord," she said quietly, after one long breath. My wife then proceeded to offer me comfort, she who had just received a sentence far rougher than my own. She assured me of her love for God, of her and Blake's love for me, and that they would be there, waiting, no matter how long I was in prison. And she reminded me that the troubles of the present were nothing to compare to the happy times we'd have later.

There were two other sets of reactions, however, to the Parole Board's decision. Within the prison, there was, frankly, a glorification of my craftiness and wrongdoing. I'd become a sort of hero. Because of the new sentencing regulations enacted prior to my confinement, I had one of the longer sentences at Eglin. The Parole Board had just clobbered me, which meant I was a legitimate and a "stand-up guy." I surely hadn't turned over evidence on another to lessen my sentence. Also, if the board had me "maxing out" for a white-collar crime on an already stiff sentence, I must have been one smart cookie on the outside. My crime must have been *big*. Inside Eglin, I'd become officially "okay." Even The Butcher looked at me with new respect.

Outside, however, the mood was different. What had happened? they asked, on the phone and by letter. Was there something I hadn't told my brothers in Christ? Had I really come to grips with my guilt and the nature of my crimes? Also, some suggested, since the Lord hadn't answered our prayers, obviously I must be doing something wrong. For some reason perhaps I wasn't meeting the conditions needed to receive a blessing. Letters offered Scriptures and lovingly suggested that I reassess my relationship with God.

The doubts of these fellow believers hurt, of course, but I could understand their viewpoint. I wished I were innocent of the crimes I'd committed. That would establish a wonderful rallying point for my prayer partners since it would be easy to pray that justice be done. It's much harder to admit that justice *was* done, and that what I was praying for was *mercy*.

Eventually, my Christian brothers and sisters were solidly behind me again. And, although we didn't see it coming, the Lord was about to use them in ways none of us had visualized. Carbon copies of letters began to arrive—letters that had been sent to the Parole Board in support of my Regional Appeal. They were requesting en masse that my sentence be cut. Soon I'd lost count of the number. After several months of this, the voice of my case worker came over the loudspeaker, summoning me to his office.

He had received an order from the regional parole board offices in Atlanta that stated that they fully agreed with the aggravating aspect of my crime, but nevertheless saw no reason to go outside the sentencing guidelines formulated by the federal government. These guidelines are based on the dollar amount of the crime, along with many other factors. According to this formula, my incarceration should have been anywhere between 24-36 months. Consequently, the regional parole board had reduced my sentence from sixty-four months to thirty-six!

It was a great moment that afternoon when I shared my good news with our prayer group and felt their joy in how God had come to my help. Each of these men had encouraged me and prayed for me. Now we all knelt together and asked God's blessings on those men and women on the outside who had given their love so generously on my behalf.

Chapter 19

Prison Fellowship

John Wilkin and I sat amidst our prayer group. Every man there could have been envious, yet they rejoiced for us. After all, we were the two guys of twelve who were picked out of an entire federal prison system that contains three hundred thousand to attend a two-week, paid seminar conducted by Prison Fellowship. We would be free men for the entire time, operating within an honor system. There'd be no guards, no bedside checks or counts.

From Eglin, John and I flew into Pittsburgh, with a two-hour layover in Atlanta. Harvey and Blake were there for a visit that was amazingly natural. It became obvious, as Blake and I played, that the miles and our separation hadn't diminished our love and affection.

It was the same with Harvey and me. I was so proud of her. She handled her challenges with a magnificent attitude. Indeed, many have said Harvey's daily walk was an example to them; they claimed that they never saw her with bowed head or unsmiling face. She praised God for her blessings, showed a forgiving spirit, and rejoiced rather than complained. She was serving as both mother *and* father to a lively youngster who needed quality time, and I knew that Blake's great attitude toward me stemmed from the fact that his mother never displayed anything less. As she remembers:

I watched Blake and Stephen play and enjoy each other. It was a wonderful tonic for me every bit as much as it was for Blake. Stephen was the same person I had always known and admired, yet he was different. He was stronger and had more leadership qualities than I had ever seen in him before. His faith was strong; he buoyed me when he called or wrote. I felt his strength much more now than I had in the old days when the world said we had everything.

Many friendships from that affluent past had vanished. However, some of our old friends did care enough to call—at least the men did. Three married men who had known Stephen and me for years offered to help me through the lonely times I was obviously experiencing by suggesting we meet for dinner, or that I travel with them while they were out of town on business. I didn't mention any of this to Stephen; it would only have increased his torment. For the time being I would keep it to myself. I wasn't bitter, just disappointed. I could see how much these men needed a living God in their lives, too, just as Stephen and I had. But I didn't feel that taking them on as ministry projects was part of God's plan for my life.

Stephen had to live one day at a time, and so would I. We had discussed the dynamics of prison life—aspects that were his and his alone to handle. And, without him at home, I was in a prison, too. There were some things that were only mine to handle.

At Pittsburg, John and I joined seven other inmates from elsewhere around the country. We piled into a Prison Fellowship van and began the hour-long drive to the Ligonier Valley Study Center in Stahlstown, Pennsylvania. There we were housed two to a room in a beautiful chalet with suites opening into a great room and fire in the huge fireplace.

This is where we had our classes and enjoyed fellowship while relishing our freedom.

We found the staff to be quite fascinating, as well as interested in us. This was their first experience with inmates, and they genuinely were excited to have us as guests for the week. Sometimes we ate in the dining hall, but often we were invited into the teachers' homes, where we enjoyed delicious meals amid warm family surroundings.

It wasn't all study. There was a ski trip at a nearby lodge—a hilarious excursion—the highlight being my rather spectacular crash into a tool shed. The laughter and kidding I took that day were unmerciful!

Another evening we visited a Pizza Hut—an unimaginable treat for guys who'd eaten prison food as long as we had. We ordered the works, ate like condemned men, and luxuriated in simply sitting at a table and enjoying waitress service.

"I hope everything was okay," our waitress commented as she presented our checks.

"Great!" answered one of the guys.

"Are you men from around these parts?"

"No, we're in town one week and staying at the Ligonier Valley Study Center."

"That's nice. Is it a convention? What business are you in?"

"You might say we work for the government," said Al*, who was doing time for second-degree murder.

"Well, enjoy your stay. I hope the service was okay."

"Ma'am, I want you to know something very honestly," Al continued. "This is the best service I've had in the past ten years!"

As our waitress floated away, thrilled over the compliment, we couldn't begin to stifle our laughter.

Our week at Ligonier passed all too quickly. We'd become a close-knit group by now, bound together by good teaching, Bible study, prayer, and fellowship. It was hard to say good-bye. We chipped in and bought red roses for the ladies on staff; they were tearfully given and tearfully received.

The second week was spent in Washington, D.C., where we were housed at the Holy Name Monastery. We had private rooms and use of the upstairs kitchen. How wonderful to have snack privileges! For days we studied. Each evening, however, we visited various area churches where we gave personal testimonies and fellowshipped with local congregations. I was treated to so many poultry dinners that even today I have a hard time passing a Kentucky Fried Chicken without having an overwhelming desire to witness.

That Sunday I gave my testimony at the Fourth Presbyterian Church in Bethesda, Maryland. Two thousand people attended each service, and a short part of my testimony was used on a local radio program. Days later, at our graduation ceremony, a man sought me out, threw his arms around me, and began to cry. He told me he had asked Jesus into his life many years earlier, but for the past fifteen years had backslid and hardly ever visited church. My short testimony on the radio had brought him to his knees, and he had rededicated his life to God.

This story dumbfounded me. Upon my return to Eglin, however, I received many letters with similar reports. It made me realize how hungry people are to hear the Good News, and it reminded me of two truths from Scripture: "Blessed are those who come in the name of the Lord," and "The crops are plentiful, but the laborers are few."

Harvey was able to join me for our final two days of the seminar. The Pattersons surprised us by giving Harvey a plane ticket to Washington, and our sweet friend Grace

Kinser provided funds for our hotel room and miscellaneous expenses. Prison Fellowship had received permission from the Bureau of Prisons for husbands and wives to stay in a downtown Washington motel the last two days and provided free time within our schedules. Harvey and I took lovely walks in the snow and long lunches where we could talk and catch up. We were amazed how, after thirteen years of marriage and the events of recent years, we still enjoyed one another so much.

It was hard to imagine, as we sat and talked, that I was a federal prisoner. Nothing seemed any different, yet in two days we'd both return to our confinements.

Commencement exercises were emotional and unforgettable. I'd been chosen to give a three-minute overview of our two weeks in Washington and Ligonier, but had not prepared any notes. Anyway, the snow was coming down hard; attendance probably would be light.

We walked into the church and found it jammed. People were seated in the aisles and in the choir loft behind the pulpit. When the program began and I was introduced, I started my talk by saying that Chuck Colson had asked me to limit my remarks to three minutes.

"Well, I have no intention of doing that," I told them. "I'll speak as long as I'd like. After all, what can he do to me? Throw me in prison?"

Laughter and applause broke out everywhere. After a few moments of serious comments, I prepared to conclude my talk. At that moment, I noticed the look on Harvey's face. She was proud of me, a convict. Lord knows, I couldn't take my eyes off her.

"Honey, I love you so much," I said out loud. "There isn't a day that goes by that I don't thank God for you. I praise God that you have forgiven me, just as Jesus has done. I'm very blessed." Then, to the crowd, I continued, "I hope the Lord blesses each of you and the families you represent, richly and without limit—as he has mine."

That moment remains one of the highest in my life—when I was able to tell my wife publicly how much I loved and appreciated her.

The final ceremonies left us all at a high emotional level. We had been the center of attention and the object of many, many prayers. It would be hard to return to prison, where the distaste of the guards was so automatic.

Harvey and I departed for Atlanta the following morning. I wasn't due back at Eglin until evening, so we had a precious opportunity to attend church and worship together as a family. Following services, there were countless hellos, kisses, and handshakes during the fellowship period. The day passed joyously, but all too quickly. At the airport later, I kissed Harvey and Blake good-bye, then boarded the plane to return to prison.

The flight to Eglin was quick, and soon one of the guards greeted me, asked how I'd enjoyed my two weeks, walked me to the back room, and began the customary strip search.

I was home.

Chapter 20

From Family to Family

In Washington I had met Norman Carlson, Director of the Bureau of Prisons, and Ben Malcolm, the National Parole Board director. These men, impressed with Prison Fellowship's accomplishments, always invited seminar members to their offices for fellowship and questions. Ben Malcolm particularly impressed me. When some of us asked questions that permitted him to share his faith, he seized the opportunity. His testimony was modestly told, touching, and very believable.

We had also enjoyed getting to know Chuck Colson and his wife Patty. Chuck had offered his help in any way possible during my appeal process. He could hardly have known how timely his invitation was. One of the first things I had to accomplish upon returning to Eglin was writing my Washington appeal.

The day I sat down at the typewriter I ended up writing pages of what I can only call my testimony. How else could I explain to these people the change that had come to my life? As a pauper in prison, I now had the peace and joy that I never had as as "successful" man on the outside. I had failed miserably at success but had succeeded during failure because of Jesus' love for me. Why else would I be fit to be a free citizen, if Jesus Christ hadn't transformed me from the inside? When the project was finished, I decided that either the parole committee would consider me crazy or the Holy Spirit would leap off the page and seize each of their hearts.

Next, I wrote a letter to all the people who had supported me for so long back home, and to those new friends I'd met on my recent trip, and requested assistance via their recommendations to the authorities.

Response to this letter was overwhelming. Letters written on my behalf poured into the various offices I'd named. Exactly ninety-four days from the time I posted my appeal, I was summoned to my case manager's office.

I looked at the form in his hand; I had received a twelve-month cut. Better than that, I had been recommended for a halfway house. A halfway house is a place in a person's home town (in my case, an old Salvation Army boarding facility) where the prisoner stays for a set period of time. He is still a federal prisoner. He checks in at night but can hold a day job and gets weekends free. Thus, it is a halfway point between the person and real freedom, helping him to adjust to normal responsibilites and the outside world. I applied for a six-month halfway house, which is unusual—the customary time is a few weeks. But the six-month stay was approved. I would be able to spend Christmas with my family. In all, I would only be at Eglin for eighteen months.

Chaplain Castillo invited me to preach on my final Sunday, and I accepted with great pleasure. Harvey and Blake came down for the service and to say good-bye to friends we'd grown to love and respect. Carol*, a friend to all in the prison fellowship from the First Baptist Church, came to sing. Our choir also sang a few hymns, and Chaplain Castillo gave me an especially generous introduction. Following my sermon, several answered the invitation to ask Jesus to come into their lives. The service concluded with our Chapel Choir singing a personal favorite of mine, "Because He Lives, I Can Face Tomorrow." It was hard to say goodbye to the chaplain; we had logged a lot of prayer hours together.

Four days later came my last prayer group meeting. It was somewhat like a time of eulogy, with my brothers in Christ saying many touching things to me. It's amazing how, in such a harsh place as prison, the hearts of men can become tender and vulnerable. And I know it only happens by the grace of God.

Bill Bever's sentence had been reduced to forty months, so I would soon see him on the outside, too. The following morning I left on a commercial bus destined to arrive in Atlanta late that afternoon. I'd been given a bus ticket and thirty dollars in cash, compliments of my favorite Bureau of Prisons. But I passed on the green leisure suit; Harvey had provided clothes for this day: September 5, 1980.

As the bus droned out the miles toward Atlanta, I wondered what the future would bring. Would I ever again be successful in business? Would people come to trust me? Would my life again be normal? Time would tell. I knew that the Lord's main concern was the condition of my heart. And my heart held the knowledge that I had been cleansed and forgiven.

The bus pulled into Atlanta on schedule, and soon I spotted Harvey and Blake at the top of the escalator. In moments I had reached them. The three of us crowded close for a corporate hug. After a long embrace with Harvey, I picked up my almost-seven-year-old son, who was much taller and heavier than when I left.

Before anything else, I had to report to my halfway house. I was still a federal prisoner, and would be for six more months. Processing went quickly at the halfway facility. They allowed me to check out for the weekend until eleven o'clock Sunday evening, which is the normal policy. I was free to go home!

Harvey drove, and Blake sat on my lap. "Stephen, it's over. It's really over, isn't it?" Harvey and I were both amazed that suddenly our lives seemed ordinary again.

"Yes, Honey, it is."

"Daddy, I have a soccer game Saturday. It's the first game of the season. Will you come?"

"Are you kidding? I wouldn't miss it for anything!"

"When we get home will you play ball with me in the yard?" Blake was full of words now, news and questions he had stored up since I had left. Uncle Tim had gone with him for Father's Day at school the year before, but would I be there next time? Did I know he could catch a football now? He played soccer last year, but didn't score any goals. Well, he did score, but it was the wrong goal. Could I coach him some?

I was conscious of every moment: Blake sitting on my lap, his little body next to mine; holding his hand while my other arm hugged his waist; feeling Harvey's hand resting on my left leg; sneaking little kisses on Blake's neck and cheek. God was already in the process of restoring those years the locusts had eaten (Joel 2:25).

Traffic was heavy, but finally we exited the expressway. Out of words at last (and shushed somewhat by Harvey), Blake relaxed and became a third party to the conversation Harvey and I had begun. "How do you feel, Stephen? Is it strange?"

"Strangely enough, no. It's hard to believe that I'm just a few hours away from prison. I guess you and Blake are easy to come home to." I laughed, squeezing her hand.

My mind was operating on several levels at once. Outside, the old familiar streets slid by, looking just the same, yet different. My son in my arms was warm and solid, yet older, heavier, his legs suddenly longer.

Harvey, though. Ah, she'd stayed the same. When I looked at her, I still saw the beautiful actress and dancer I met in New York City all those years ago.

My background involved working as a ballet dancer, actress, model, and spokesperson, she once wrote. *I received praise for my performances, beauty, and the next big job around the corner. I was highly motivated to achieve, to be successful, to be a winner in other people's eyes. My worth was based on my accomplishments . . .*

No longer, I thought.

"You look different," she was saying to me.

"What do you mean?"

"You have an intensity in your face I never saw before. You have a furrow between your eyes, too. And there's something different from the old Steve Lawson. I don't see the same bravado and self-confidence. But still, in another way, you're stronger than ever."

I listened, nodding in agreement, watching all that was happening on famous old Peachtree Street. Just two or three miles behind us, yet in another way so far behind us, was that funny little apartment where we'd begun our life together. We'd come a long way since the day we stood at the window, catching the end of the rainbow in the palms of our outstretched hands.

"Do you remember—" I started to ask, but then Harvey approached Vermont Road and began that final left turn as I caught my breath. We were moving into our driveway, and my eyes drank in every detail.

I saw the trees . . . the bushes . . . every twig in our yard . . . through rainbows created by my tears. The yellow ribbons tied everywhere. They were just yellow ribbons;

scraps of yellow to someone else, perhaps. But to my daz-zled eyes that moment, they were a vision, even a revela-tion.

We were home. We were together. Suddenly I'd found something I never believed in before, or thought was pos-sible to see. I had found the pot of gold at the end of the rainbow.

Epilogue

Home. I had come home to my family. All the daydreams, prayers, and hopes came to fruition. After eighteen months at Eglin Prison, I was where I belonged and wanted to be. I had assumed that the three of us would have adjustments to make, but the transition was surprisingly smooth.

However, it wasn't long before I realized how difficult my time away had been for Blake. Suddenly he had a father who corrected him, whereas before he had regarded Harvey as his sole authority figure. Now there was someone else competing for time with his mother; he had to share her with me. Gradually though, my life became enmeshed in their daily routines once again.

After my release, I became the state director of Georgia for Prison Fellowship, the ministry begun by Chuck Colson. This position included coordinating the many volunteers coming into prison ministry. I sought opportunities to tell people who needed to hear it most what Jesus Christ had done in my life.

Later I became the manager of National Accounts for Days Inn of America. I had started my search for God in a Days Inn motel room in Gainesville, Florida, when I had been there during my business trip and picked up the Bible. During the time I worked for that chain, they passed a significant milestone: they gave away their four millionth Bible.

Until those two positions, I went through lengthy periods of unemployment. I went through the normal process of job seeking—filling out applications, making numerous phone calls, and answering almost every ad in the paper that sounded remotely possible. Full disclosure of my background provided each prospective employer with the details of my past. Since I no longer lived by "situational ethics," I determined to be completely up-front. It might take a Christian with a large heart to take a chance with the likes of me, but they had the right to know all the facts.

It came as no surprise that prospective employers didn't consider me a hot property. I was now in my mid-forties, had an unfavorable credit record, and had recently come out of prison.

In desperation, I finally got a job at a parking lot. I did clean-up—sweeping, hauling out trash, and tending the booth that guarded the entrance. Each morning I started at 6:30 and got off at 2:30. But it was a job; I was employed. After that work was over for the day, I put in hours at an office-moving company in the afternoons, evenings, and weekends.

Not a lot of money came in from my working, but we got by. Harvey continued in her job, which brought in more money than my combined employment. We didn't mind, though, because we were together. We were a family again. And my relationship with Blake slowly bridged the eighteen-month gap. I became a full-time father again.

Because I worked two jobs, both demanding a lot of physical energy, coming home meant I could put my feet up and relax. I especially liked to collapse on the sofa and read, soaking in the atmosphere of our apartment.

Frequently Blake would come into the room just as I settled down. "Hey, Daddy, want to throw a football around?"

In truth, I didn't want to get off the sofa. Then I would remember all the times I lay on my cot in prison, asking God to provide again meaningful opportunities to be with Blake. "Sure, Son, let's do that." And the two of us would throw ourselves into play on the front lawn, tossing and tackling. Blake was growing up, and I no longer gave him the piggy-back rides as I had when he was four or five. But the form of play didn't matter; we were together.

The past was past; I had broken the law and served my time in prison. Nevertheless, my problems had taken their toll.

Blake's first-grade teacher sent home a note: *Blake is not doing well in school.* She set up a meeting with Harvey and me. Mrs. Bradshaw* told us that Blake's grades were suffering because of his lack of deportment. She concluded that he acted out his frustrations and problems by attempting to attract attention. He did get the attention he wanted, only it was negative attention.

A few minutes into the meeting, she called Blake into the room. She gave him her most professional smile and paused. "Your parents and I have had a discussion about you, your work, and the fact that you have continued to be disruptive in the classroom."

Blake dropped his gaze. He was seated between Harvey and me, with Mrs. Bradshaw across the desk in front of us. I sensed his apprehension and put a hand on his shoulder, but he didn't look up.

As Mrs. Bradshaw talked on and described his behavior, Blake furtively glanced at her, then at his mother. Finally he dropped his head, obviously ashamed and defeated. Then

Mrs. Bradshaw began to question him, citing the wrongs he had committed and asking him in each case, "Is that true, Blake?" or something to that effect. I could see what she was trying to do—get him to acknowledge what he had done—but it began to feel like a criminal hearing. After a while, just as Blake began to cry, I had to interrupt.

"Mrs. Bradshaw, I hope you don't mind, but I have something to say."

"Certainly, Mr. Lawson." She smiled appreciatively.

"As you know, Mrs. Bradshaw, I made mistakes when I was operating my real estate investment firm. You're aware that I spent eighteen months in prison. Because of all the events that led up to that tragedy, I became a Christian. I received God's forgiveness because he loved me in spite of the poor choices I had made—"

Mrs. Bradshaw appeared to be uncomfortable with my talk about prison. She tried to interrupt, but I tightened my grip on Blake's shoulder and continued. Blake had stopped crying and was looking at me.

"Blake had to learn early in life that even daddies make mistakes. That's a hard lesson for a boy so young to learn. Knowing God's forgiveness has totally changed my life. But, frankly, if Blake hadn't forgiven me I don't know if I could have lived. When he was five years old, he forgave me for all the wrong things I had done, and for abandoning him by going to prison. He forgave me for the shame I brought to him. I know he suffered the taunts of other children because of where I was.

"He forgave me when I couldn't be with him for the Father-and-Son day here at school. I couldn't be with him on his birthday and Christmas. He visited me in prison—out of love. I didn't deserve the kind of loyalty Blake gave to me. He loved me when I least deserved it."

I turned to Blake then, and, choking back emotion, said, "I'm trying to say that I love you, Son. Just as you forgive me for all the wrong things I've done, I forgive you for everything you've done up to this moment. The slate is wiped clean."

I couldn't say anymore. I glanced at Harvey and her smile confirmed that I had done the right thing. I hadn't spoken loudly or in anger. The words had come out softly because they were a mixture of joy and pain.

To her credit, Mrs. Bradshaw sat in silence. The professionalism vanished, and her eyes told me that she had witnessed something unusual—forgiveness taking place. I'm sure she didn't have these kind of parent-teacher conferences on a regular basis.

Dear Harvey broke the silence by turning to Blake. "Is there anything you would like to tell Mrs. Bradshaw?"

He nodded and took a deep breath. "I'm sorry, Mrs. Bradshaw. I'm really sorry. I promise to be a better boy. Will you . . . forgive me?"

"Oh, yes, Blake. Yes! And . . . will you forgive me, too? I realize that I haven't been as nice toward you as I could have been. I'm sorry, too."

"Oh, that's okay."

We all laughed nervously, not sure how to exit from such an intense few moments.

"Blake, your dad mentioned that daddies make mistakes," Mrs. Bradshaw said, her eyes glistening. "I have to be honest enough to say that teachers make mistakes as well."

As we left the building, Blake ran out the door and took a short cut across the wet lawn and reached the car first. Harvey and I watched him while we followed, hand-in-hand. He stood at the door, beaming at us.

I wanted to say a hundred things to my son in that moment. He had shown such maturity and compassion in the past eighteen months. I gave him a hug. "Come on, Son, let's all go for a milkshake!"

Eleven years have passed since that incident. Blake is still not perfect. Nor am I. We both prove that daily. But we forgive and go on.

Since late 1984 I have been in business for myself. Again the Lord has proven faithful. Two months after I started my business, Harvey quit her job. She had carried the family for a long time, and it was my turn to take over the finances.

I realize that I've made a lot of mistakes. But three things continue to encourage me and let me know that I am loved and forgiven.

First, God's love and forgiveness has become deeply real to me in the years since 1978.

Second, the relationship between Harvey and me has continued to mature. Our love stands stronger than ever.

Finally, I have a son, now a brother in Christ, who knows that daddies make mistakes. In spite of my clay feet, he loves me, understands, and forgives.

Dear Reader,

My prayer has constantly been that God will use this book to touch many lives and to give hope.

I pray that my story has encouraged you. Perhaps, like me, you've wanted to turn over a new leaf in life but have found that a new leaf isn't all that you need—you need a *new life*. You want to be different—from the inside. You're tired of constantly striving to make yourself "acceptable." You are exhausted with having to deal with your life's past decisions and actions.

When I first read Jesus' words, "Come to me, all you who are weary and burdened, and I will give you rest" (Matthew 11:28) and "Peace I leave with you; my peace I give you. I do not give to you as the world gives. Do not let your hearts be troubled and do not be afraid" (John 14:27), I knew with certainty that God understood exactly what I needed and that he knew me well—from the inside out. All I ever wanted in my life was to experience rest and peace. To never again be lonely. To know a living God who would always be faithful, sufficient, forgiving, merciful, and just.

Do I speak what is in *your* heart? If so, please join me in this prayer:

Heavenly Father,
In the best way I know how I ask that you come into my heart and take over my life. I realize that I need you. Please change my life. Help me to see with new eyes and to hear with new ears. I open the door of my heart to you. Thank you for forgiving my sins. Make me the kind of person you want me to be. Thank you for hearing my prayer and allowing me to know you as Savior and Lord. In Jesus your Son's name,
Amen.

If you have prayed this prayer, you are now my new brother or sister in the Lord. How I would appreciate hearing from you. Would you take the time to write? If so, I promise to reply. May the Lord bless you and the family you represent, richly and without limit.

In His Peace & Joy,

Steve Lawson

Stephen P. Lawson
c/o Partners In Travel, Inc.
Northlake Quandrangle
2200 Northlake Parkway
Suite 275
Tucker, GA 30084

The author or his family receive no remuneration from the proceeds of the sale of this book. Proceeds are given, as unto the Lord, to Prison Fellowship, Washington, D.C. 20041-0500.